CONTEMPORARY'S
REAL NUMBERS
Developing Thinking Skills in Math
Algebra Basics

Allan D. Suter

Project Editor
Kathy Osmus

CB
CONTEMPORARY
BOOKS
CHICAGO

Published by Contemporary Books, Inc.
180 North Michigan Avenue, Chicago, Illinois 60601
Manufactured in the United States of America
International Standard Book Number: 0-8092-4209-5

Published simultaneously in Canada by
Fitzhenry & Whiteside
91 Granton Drive
Richmond Hill, Ontario L4B 2N5
Canada

Editorial Director
Caren Van Slyke

Editorial
Lisa Black
Ellen Frechette
Laura Larson
Leah Mayes
Steve Miller
Bonnie Needham
Robin O'Connor
Betsy Rubin
Seija Suter

Editorial Assistant
Erica Pochis

Editorial Production Manager
Norma Fioretti

Production Editor
Marina Micari

Cover Design
Lois Stein

Illustrator
Cliff Hayes

Art & Production
Carolyn Hopp

Typography
Impressions, Inc.
Madison, Wisconsin

Cover photo © by Michael Slaughter

CONTENTS

1 EXPRESSIONS, VARIABLES, AND EQUATIONS
Words to Expressions 1
Identify the Unknown 2
Variables 3
Learning about Equations 4

2 ADDITION AND SUBTRACTION EQUATIONS
Relating Addition and Subtraction 5
Equations and Balance Scales 6
Solving Equations 7
Inverse Operations 8
Solving Equations by Adding or Subtracting 9
Equations to Add or Subtract 10
Sentences to Equations 11

3 MULTIPLICATION AND DIVISION EQUATIONS
Relating Multiplication and Division 12
Solving Equations by Dividing 13
Solving Equations by Multiplying 14
Equations to Multiply or Divide 15
Word Statements to Equations 16
Proportion 17
Proportions in Problem Solving 18
Mixed Practice 19
Define a Variable 20
Problem-Solving Skills 21

4 TWO-STEP EQUATIONS
Two-Step Equations Using a Balance Scale 22
Picture the Equations 23
Solving Two-Step Equations 24
More Two-Step Equations 25
Checking Two-Step Equations 26
Translating Word Statements 27
More Problem Solving 28
Review Your Skills 29

5 INTEGER ADDITION AND SUBTRACTION

Negative and Positive Numbers 30
Use the Number Line 31
Comparing and Ordering Integers 32
Adding Integers with the Same Sign 33
Adding Integers with Different Signs 34
Absolute Value 35
Rules for Adding Integers 36
Subtracting Integers with the Same Sign 37
Relating Subtraction to Addition 38
Using Opposites 39
Rules for Subtracting Integers 40
Adding and Subtracting Integers 41
Applications Using Integers 42

6 INTEGER MULTIPLICATION AND DIVISION

Multiplying Integers with Different Signs 43
Multiplying Integers with the Same Sign 44
Multiplying Integers 45
Dividing Integers with Different Signs 46
Dividing Integers with the Same Sign 47
Dividing Integers 48
Review of Integers 49
Applications Using Integers 50
Multistep Problems Using Integers 51

7 ORDER OF OPERATIONS

Learning Order of Operations 52
Ordering Expressions 53
Simplify the Expression 54
Using Order of Operation 55
Exponents 56
Evaluate Expressions 57
Evaluate with Exponents 58
Review Your Skills 59

8 FORMULAS

Learning about Formulas 60
Using Formulas 61
Simple Interest 62
Time, Rate, and Distance 63
Geometric Formulas 64

9 ORDERED PAIRS

Learning about Ordered Pairs 65
More Ordered Pairs 66
Graphing Ordered Pairs 67

ANSWER KEY 68

Words to Expressions

It is often necessary to change word expressions to **mathematical expressions.** Key words frequently used to write word expressions and their symbols are listed below.

Key Words and Their Symbols			
Term	**Symbol**	**Term**	**Symbol**
plus	+	minus	−
add	+	subtract	−
sum	+	times	×
more	+	product	×
increase	+	divide	÷
greater	+	quotient	÷
less	−	equal	=
difference	−	is	=

▶ Change each word expression to a mathematical expression.

1. Nine more than six $\underline{\quad 6 + 9 \quad}$

2. Sixty-four divided by eight $\underline{\qquad}$

3. The product of six and four $\underline{\qquad}$

4. Six less than fifteen $\underline{\qquad}$

5. The sum of fifteen and twenty $\underline{\qquad}$

6. The difference between seven and three $\underline{\qquad}$

▶ Write a word expression for each mathematical expression.

7. $10 - 7$ _____

8. 9×2 _____

9. $4 + 3$ _____

10. $15 \div 3$ _____

11. 20×5 _____

12. $18 + 9$ _____

13. $56 \div 8$ _____

14. $13 - 5$ _____

Identify the Unknown

▶ Sometimes word expressions contain **unknown** values. Circle the unknown value in each word expression.

Example: (Larry's sales) decreased by $550. (You don't know the value of *Larry's sales*.)

1. Five more than (a number) (You don't know the value of *a number*.)

2. Kevin paid $28 plus tax for two shirts. (You don't know how much *tax* was paid.)

3. Six divided by a number

4. Refunds decreased by $195.

5. Seven multiplied by a number

6. Judy's commission increased by $1,275.

7. The sale price plus $2.75 in taxes

8. A salesman sold a new car for $17,980 plus options.

9. Eight subtracted from some number

10. A number times nine

Variables

Algebra uses letters (*x, y, z, n, a,* etc.) to stand for unknown numbers. These letters are called **variables.**

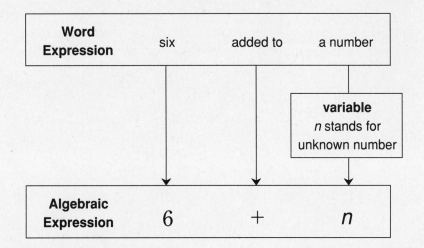

▶ Any letter may be used as a variable. For each word expression, circle the unknown. Then, choose a variable and write an algebraic expression.

1. Three less than (a number)　　$n - 3$

2. An amount increased by five dollars ＿＿＿＿＿＿

3. The sum of fourteen and some number ＿＿＿＿＿＿

4. Twenty decreased by a number ＿＿＿＿＿＿

5. Mary's traveling time plus one hour ＿＿＿＿＿＿

6. Ten adults and some students ＿＿＿＿＿＿

7. Thirty cents added to the cost of a pencil ＿＿＿＿＿＿

8. A number divided by nine ＿＿＿＿＿＿

9. A weight decreased by two pounds ＿＿＿＿＿＿

10. Five times a number ＿＿＿＿＿＿

Learning about Equations

Equations can be shown with pictures. An **equation** shows that two amounts are equal.

Algebraic Equation	**Picture**

$$n + 3 = 8$$
(A number plus 3 equals 8.)

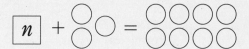

▶ Write an equation for each picture.

1.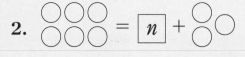

_____
equation

3.

_____
equation

2.

_____
equation

4.

_____
equation

An algebraic expression that includes the equal symbol (=) is called an **equation.**

▶ Write an algebraic equation.

equals

5. Six plus a number is ten.

_____
equation

6. A number minus six is three.

_____
equation

7. 9 times some number is 18.

_____
equation

8. A number divided by three is seven.

_____
equation

▶ Write each equation using words.

9. $x + 4 = 5$

_____

10. $a - 3 = 10$

_____

11. $4 \times b = 12$

_____

12. $9 = n + 1$

_____

Relating Addition and Subtraction

You may remember that you can write a subtraction equation based on an addition equation or an addition equation based on a subtraction equation.

Example A: If $6 - 2 = 4$, then you know that $2 + 4 = 6$.

Example B: If $9 + 8 = 17$, then you know that $17 - 8 = 9$.

▶ Use the relationship between addition and subtraction to complete the chart.

	Numbers	Addition Equation	Subtraction Equation
1.	17, 4, 21	$\underline{17} + 4 = 21$	$21 - 4 = \underline{\quad}$
2.	11, 23, 34	$11 + 23 = \underline{\quad}$	$\underline{\quad} - 23 = \underline{\quad}$
3.	49, 22, 27	$27 + \underline{\quad} = \underline{\quad}$	$49 - \underline{\quad} = 22$
4.	12, 5, 7	$\underline{\quad} + \underline{\quad} = 12$	$\underline{\quad} - \underline{\quad} = 5$
5.	5, 9, 14	$\underline{\quad} + 9 = \underline{\quad}$	$\underline{\quad} - 9 = \underline{\quad}$
6.	76, 165, 89	$76 + \underline{\quad} = \underline{\quad}$	$165 - \underline{\quad} = 89$
7.	425, 138, 287	$\underline{\quad} + 138 = \underline{\quad}$	$\underline{\quad} - 138 = \underline{\quad}$

▶ For each group of numbers, write an addition equation and a related subtraction equation.

8. 4, 6, 10

$\underline{4 + 6 = 10}$ $\underline{10 - 6 = 4}$
    addition   subtraction

10. 10, 30, 20

$\underline{\hspace{3cm}}$ $\underline{\hspace{3cm}}$
    addition   subtraction

9. 7, 15, 22

$\underline{\hspace{3cm}}$ $\underline{\hspace{3cm}}$
    addition   subtraction

11. 101, 64, 37

$\underline{\hspace{3cm}}$ $\underline{\hspace{3cm}}$
    addition   subtraction

Equations and Balance Scales

The equal sign in an equation tells you that both sides have the same value. Think of an equation as a balanced scale. Both sides must be equal for the scale to balance.

Example

To write a balanced equation, simply list what is shown on each side of the scale. Remember to balance the equation around an equal sign.

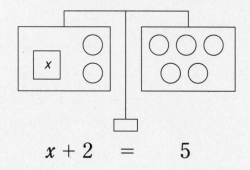

$$x + 2 \quad = \quad 5$$

▶ Use each drawing to write an equation.

1.

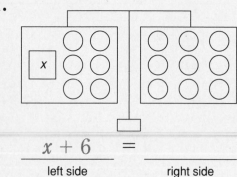

$$\underline{\quad x + 6 \quad} = \underline{\quad\quad\quad}$$
left side   right side

3.

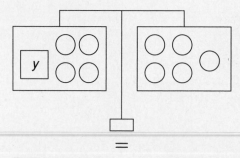

$$\underline{\quad\quad\quad} = \underline{\quad\quad\quad}$$
left side   right side

2.

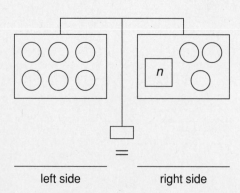

$$\underline{\quad\quad\quad} = \underline{\quad\quad\quad}$$
left side   right side

4.

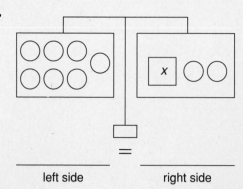

$$\underline{\quad\quad\quad} = \underline{\quad\quad\quad}$$
left side   right side

Solving Equations

To solve an equation, find the value of the variable to make the equation true.

▶ Use each drawing to help you write an equation and solve it.

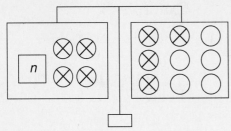

1. a) $\underline{\quad n + 4 \quad}$ = $\underline{\quad 9 \quad}$

   b) To get *n* alone, remove

      $\underline{\quad 4 \quad}$ circles from the left side.

   c) To keep the balance, remove

      $\underline{\quad 4 \quad}$ circles from the right side.

   d) *n* = $\underline{\qquad}$
      circles left

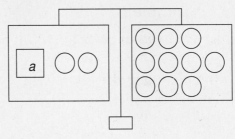

3. a) $\underline{\qquad\qquad}$ = $\underline{\qquad\qquad}$

   b) To get *a* alone, remove

      $\underline{\qquad}$ circles from the left side.

   c) To keep the balance, remove

      $\underline{\qquad}$ circles from the right side.

   d) *a* = $\underline{\qquad}$

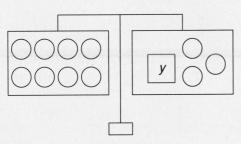

2. a) $\underline{\qquad\qquad}$ = $\underline{\qquad\qquad}$

   b) To get *y* alone, remove

      $\underline{\qquad}$ circles from the right side.

   c) To keep the balance, remove

      $\underline{\qquad}$ circles from the left side.

   d) *y* = $\underline{\qquad}$

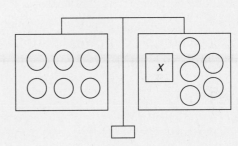

4. a) $\underline{\qquad\qquad}$ = $\underline{\qquad\qquad}$

   b) To get *x* alone, remove

      $\underline{\qquad}$ circles from the right side.

   c) To keep the balance, remove

      $\underline{\qquad}$ circles from the left side.

   d) *x* = $\underline{\qquad}$

▶ Solve each equation by finding the value of the variable.

5. $y + 7 = 10$

   $y =$ $\underline{\qquad}$
      solution

6. $16 = x + 7$

   $\underline{\qquad} = x$
      solution

7. $a + 9 = 13$

   $a =$ $\underline{\qquad}$
      solution

8. $15 = t + 11$

   $\underline{\qquad} = t$
      solution

Inverse Operations

As you have discovered, addition and subtraction are **inverse** (opposite) **operations.** The examples below will show you how to apply what you have learned.

Example A

To find n, you need to get n alone.

What is happening in the equation below? 5 is being added to something to get 30.

$$n + 5 = 30$$

Since 5 is being added to n, **subtract** 5 from both sides of the equation.

Example B

To find x, you need to get x alone.

What is happening in the equation below? 8 is being subtracted from something to get 3.

$$x - 8 = 3$$

Since 8 is being subtracted from x, **add** 8 to both sides of the equation.

> Notice that whatever is done to one side of the equation, the same thing must be done to the other side to keep the equation balanced.

▶ Write the number you would subtract from each side to solve the equation.

1. $c + 8 = 12$

Subtract _____ from each side.

2. $43 = x + 18$

Subtract _____ from each side.

3. $16 + b = 57$

Subtract _____ from each side.

4. $109 = 51 + y$

Subtract _____ from each side.

5. $a + 88 = 112$

Subtract _____ from each side.

▶ Write the number you would add to each side to solve the equation.

6. $h - 19 = 8$

Add _____ to each side.

7. $27 = n - 52$

Add _____ to each side.

8. $121 = g - 17$

Add _____ to each side.

9. $n - 49 = 21$

Add _____ to each side.

10. $x - 152 = 119$

Add _____ to each side.

Solving Equations by Adding or Subtracting

Some equations can be solved by using addition or subtraction.

Example A	**Example B**
$x + 4 = 6$	$11 = y - 5$

Ask yourself, "What do I need to do to get x alone?"

Ask yourself, "What do I need to do to get y alone?"

Because 4 is being **added** to x, **subtract** 4 from both sides of the equation.

Because 5 is being **subtracted** from y, **add** 5 to both sides of the equation.

$$
\begin{aligned}
x + 4 &= 6 \\
- 4 &\;\; - 4 \\
x &= 2
\end{aligned}
$$

Subtract the same number that has been added. You get a value of 0 and the x alone.

$$
\begin{aligned}
11 &= y - 5 \\
+ 5 &\quad\;\; + 5 \\
16 &= y
\end{aligned}
$$

Add the same number that has been taken away. You get a value of 0 and the y alone.

▶ Solve the equations.

1. $y - 8 = 21$
$$+ 8 \quad + 8$$
$$y \quad = \underline{}$$

2. $a + 19 = 42$
$$\Box \quad \Box$$
$$a \quad = \underline{}$$

3. $28 = b - 13$
$$\Box \quad \Box$$
$$\underline{} = b$$

4. $c - 17 = 35$
$$\Box \quad \Box$$
$$c \quad = \underline{}$$

5. $61 \quad = x + 37$
$$\Box \quad \Box$$
$$\underline{} = x$$

6. $46 \quad = x + 29$
$$\Box \quad \Box$$
$$\underline{} = x$$

7. $a + 17 = 31$
$$\Box \quad \Box$$
$$a \quad = \underline{}$$

8. $132 \quad = a - 58$
$$\Box \quad \Box$$
$$\underline{} = a$$

Equations to Add or Subtract

It is important to **check** your answer when working with an equation. You check your work to make sure that both sides of the equation are equal.

Example A

$$t + 38 = 93 \quad \text{equation}$$
$$\underline{ - 38 \quad -38} \quad \text{Subtract.}$$
$$t = 55 \quad \text{solution}$$

Check:

$t + 38 = 93$ ← Copy the original equation.

$\mathbf{55} + 38 = 93$ ← Replace the variable (t) with the solution (55).

$93 = 93$ ← The solution is correct. Both sides are equal.

Example B

$$x - 27 = 15 \quad \text{equation}$$
$$\underline{ + 27 \quad +27} \quad \text{Add.}$$
$$x = 42 \quad \text{solution}$$

Check:

$x - 27 = 15$ ← Copy the original equation.

$\mathbf{42} - 27 = 15$ ← Replace the variable (x) with the solution (42).

$15 = 15$ ← The solution is correct. Both sides are equal.

▶ Solve each equation. Then check your solution.

1. $x - 7 = 15$

2. $30 + t = 93$

3. $a + 128 = 314$

4. $50 = h - 18$

5. $84 = r + 28$

6. $x - 172 = 86$

7. $500 = b - 50$

8. $n + 316 = 648$

Sentences to Equations

A word statement, or sentence, can be written as an equation. Remember the key words on page 1 when changing sentences to equations.

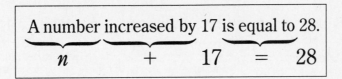

A number increased by 17 is equal to 28.
$$n + 17 = 28$$

▶ Change each word statement to an algebraic equation and solve.

1. x decreased by 15 is 9.

   a) $\underline{\quad x - 15 = 9 \quad}$
          equation

   b) $x = \underline{\quad\quad}$
          solution

2. The sum of n and 59 is 101.

   a) $\underline{\quad\quad\quad\quad\quad}$
          equation

   b) $n = \underline{\quad\quad}$
          solution

3. 65 more than x is 421.

   a) $\underline{\quad\quad\quad\quad\quad}$
          equation

   b) $x = \underline{\quad\quad}$
          solution

4. 17 is subtracted from y to equal 71.

   a) $\underline{\quad\quad\quad\quad\quad}$
          equation

   b) $y = \underline{\quad\quad}$
          solution

5. 135 added to c equals 211.

   a) $\underline{\quad\quad\quad\quad\quad}$
          equation

   b) $c = \underline{\quad\quad}$
          solution

▶ Choose a variable for the unknown number and solve the equation.

6. A number decreased by 53 is 27.

   a) $\underline{\quad\quad}$ = unknown number
      variable

   b) $\underline{\quad\quad\quad\quad\quad}$
          equation

   c) $\underline{\quad\quad\quad\quad\quad}$
          solution

7. 138 more than a number is 221.

   a) $\underline{\quad\quad}$ = unknown number
      variable

   b) $\underline{\quad\quad\quad\quad\quad}$
          equation

   c) $\underline{\quad\quad\quad\quad\quad}$
          solution

8. The sum of a number and 84 equals 128.

   a) $\underline{\quad\quad}$ = unknown number
      variable

   b) $\underline{\quad\quad\quad\quad\quad}$
          equation

   c) $\underline{\quad\quad\quad\quad\quad}$
          solution

9. Some number less 39 is 15.

   a) $\underline{\quad\quad}$ = unknown number
      variable

   b) $\underline{\quad\quad\quad\quad\quad}$
          equation

   c) $\underline{\quad\quad\quad\quad\quad}$
          solution

10. Subtract 118 from a number to get 56.

   a) $\underline{\quad\quad}$ = unknown number
      variable

   b) $\underline{\quad\quad\quad\quad\quad}$
          equation

   c) $\underline{\quad\quad\quad\quad\quad}$
          solution

Relating Multiplication and Division

You may remember that you can write a multiplication equation based on a division equation and a division equation based on a multiplication equation.

▶ Use the relationship between multiplication and division to complete the chart.

	Numbers	Multiplication Equation	Division Equation
1.	9, 8, 72	$\underline{\quad 9 \quad} \times 8 = 72$	$72 \div \underline{\quad\quad} = 8$
2.	39, 13, 3	$13 \times \underline{\quad\quad} = 39$	$\underline{\quad\quad} \div 13 = \underline{\quad\quad}$
3.	15, 105, 7	$\underline{\quad\quad} \times 7 = \underline{\quad\quad}$	$105 \div \underline{\quad\quad} = 7$
4.	4, 20, 80	$\underline{\quad\quad} \times \underline{\quad\quad} = 80$	$\underline{\quad\quad} \div \underline{\quad\quad} = 4$
5.	174, 6, 29	$29 \times \underline{\quad\quad} = 174$	$\underline{\quad\quad} \div 29 = \underline{\quad\quad}$
6.	8, 88, 11	$8 \times \underline{\quad\quad} = \underline{\quad\quad}$	$88 \div \underline{\quad\quad} = 8$
7.	48, 6, 8	$\underline{\quad\quad} \times 8 = \underline{\quad\quad}$	$\underline{\quad\quad} \div 8 = \underline{\quad\quad}$

▶ Write a related multiplication or division equation.

8. If $7 \times 4 = 28$, then you know that $28 \div \underline{\quad\quad} = \underline{\quad\quad}$.

9. If $40 \div 5 = 8$, then you know that $8 \times \underline{\quad\quad} = \underline{\quad\quad}$.

▶ For each group of numbers, write a multiplication equation and a related division equation.

10. 3, 7, 21

$\underline{3 \times 7 = 21}$ $21 \div \underline{\quad} = \underline{\quad}$
   equation   related equation

12. 108, 12, 9

$\underline{\qquad\qquad}$ $\underline{\qquad\qquad}$
   equation   related equation

11. 5, 45, 9

$\underline{\qquad\qquad}$ $\underline{\qquad\qquad}$
   equation   related equation

13. 10, 80, 8

$\underline{\qquad\qquad}$ $\underline{\qquad\qquad}$
   equation   related equation

Solving Equations by Dividing

Division is the inverse (opposite) of multiplication. Sometimes division is needed to get the variable alone.

Example: 7 times b is 28
$$7b = 28$$

Note: Multiplication can be shown in different ways.
$7 \times n \quad 7 \cdot n \quad 7n \quad 7(n)$
All of these versions mean the same thing.

Here you need to solve for b. Since b is being **multiplied** by 7, to get b alone, **divide** both sides by 7.

$7b = 28$
$\frac{7b}{7} = \frac{28}{7}$ ← This line means division, too.
$b = 4$

OR

When you divide by the same number you are multiplying by, you get the letter alone.

$7b \div 7 = 28 \div 7$
$b = 4$

▶ Write the number to divide each side by to solve the equation.

1. $4n = 16$

Divide each side by _____.

3. $12b = 144$

Divide each side by _____.

2. $48 = 8a$

Divide each side by _____.

4. $100 = 25y$

Divide each side by _____.

▶ Solve each equation. Check your solution.

5. $3c = 111$

$$\frac{3c}{\boxed{3}} = \frac{111}{\boxed{3}}$$

$c =$ _____

8. $156 = 13h$

$$\frac{156}{\square} = \frac{13h}{\square}$$

_____ $= h$

6. $90 = 15y$

$$\frac{90}{\square} = \frac{15y}{\square}$$

_____ $= y$

9. $20n = 800$

$$\frac{20n}{\square} = \frac{800}{\square}$$

$n =$ _____

7. $4x = 120$

$$\frac{4x}{\square} = \frac{120}{\square}$$

$x =$ _____

10. $9x = 171$

$$\frac{9x}{\square} = \frac{171}{\square}$$

$x =$ _____

Solving Equations by Multiplying

Multiplication is the inverse (opposite) of division.

Example: n divided by 6 is 4; $\frac{n}{6} = 4$

You need to solve for n. Since n is being **divided** by 6, to get n alone, **multiply** both sides by 6.

$$\frac{n}{6} = 4$$

When you multiply by the same number you are dividing by, you get the letter alone.

$$6 \cdot \frac{n}{6} = 4 \cdot 6$$
$$n = 24$$

A raised dot means the same thing as the multiplication symbol ($\times$).

▶ Write the number you would multiply each side by to solve the equation.

1. $\frac{y}{3} = 2$

Multiply each side by _____.

3. $\frac{b}{11} = 5$

Multiply each side by _____.

2. $9 = \frac{a}{3}$

Multiply each side by _____.

4. $3 = \frac{x}{18}$

Multiply each side by _____.

▶ Solve each equation.

5. $\frac{n}{9} = 6$

$\boxed{9} \cdot \frac{n}{9} = 6 \cdot \boxed{9}$

$n = $ _____

8. $13 = \frac{c}{8}$

$\boxed{} \cdot 13 = \frac{c}{8} \cdot \boxed{}$

_____ $= c$

6. $5 = \frac{a}{7}$

$\boxed{} \cdot 5 = \frac{a}{7} \cdot \boxed{}$

_____ $= a$

9. $\frac{r}{22} = 5$

$\boxed{} \cdot \frac{r}{22} = 5 \cdot \boxed{}$

$r = $ _____

7. $\frac{x}{12} = 3$

$\boxed{} \cdot \frac{x}{12} = 3 \cdot \boxed{}$

$x = $ _____

10. $\frac{h}{15} = 22$

$\boxed{} \cdot \frac{h}{15} = 22 \cdot \boxed{}$

$h = $ _____

Equations to Multiply or Divide

It is important to check your answer after solving an equation. You check your work to make sure that both sides of the equation are equal.

Example A

$$13a = 91 \quad \text{equation}$$
$$\frac{13a}{13} = \frac{91}{13} \quad \text{Divide.}$$
$$a = 7 \quad \text{solution}$$

Example B

$$\frac{x}{5} = 21 \quad \text{equation}$$
$$5 \cdot \frac{x}{5} = 21 \cdot 5 \quad \text{Multiply.}$$
$$x = 105 \quad \text{solution}$$

Check:

$13a = 91$ ← Copy the original equation.

$13(7) = 91$ ← Replace the variable (a) with 7.

$91 = 91$ ← Both sides are equal. The solution is correct.

Check:

$\frac{x}{5} = 21$ ← Copy the original equation.

$\frac{105}{5} = 21$ ← Replace the variable (x) with 105.

$21 = 21$ ← Both sides are equal. The solution is correct.

▶ Solve each equation. Then check your solution.

1. $6r = 138$

5. $21c = 168$

2. $8 = \frac{m}{7}$

6. $124 = \frac{w}{3}$

3. $350 = 25h$

7. $\frac{u}{9} = 9$

4. $\frac{n}{7} = 16$

8. $374 = 11s$

Word Statements to Equations

A word statement can be written as an equation. Remember the key words on page 1 when changing sentences to equations.

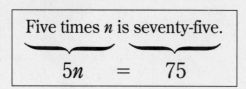

▶ Change each word statement to an algebraic equation and solve.

▶ Choose a variable for the unknown number and solve the equation.

1. 8 multiplied by *m* is 96.

  a) _____ $8m = 96$ _____
       equation

  b) $m = $ _____
       solution

2. Seventy-eight is the product of six and *r*.

  a) _____
       equation

  b) $r = $ _____
       solution

3. *x* divided by thirteen is four.

  a) _____
       equation

  b) $x = $ _____
       solution

4. 7 is the result of *t* divided by 25.

  a) _____
       equation

  b) $t = $ _____
       solution

5. 18 times *n* is 126.

  a) _____
       equation

  b) $n = $ _____
       solution

6. The product of 8 and a number is 152.

  a) _____ = unknown number
       variable

  b) _____
       equation

  c) _____
       solution

7. Some number divided by fifteen is seventy-five.

  a) _____ = unknown number
       variable

  b) _____
       equation

  c) _____
       solution

8. 135 equals a number divided by 9.

  a) _____ = unknown number
       variable

  b) _____
       equation

  c) _____
       solution

9. 23 times some number equals 253.

  a) _____ = unknown number
       variable

  b) _____
       equation

  c) _____
       solution

Proportion

A **proportion** is a statement that two **ratios** (comparisons) are equal.

When setting up a proportion, you need to decide what information is unknown. Then you need to assign (give) the unknown a variable.

Example: 5 pounds of potatoes cost $1.50. How much will 13 pounds of potatoes cost?

The first ratio compares pounds to cost.

$$\frac{5}{\$1.50} \frac{\text{pounds}}{\text{cost}} = \frac{13}{n} \frac{\text{pounds}}{\text{cost}}$$

The second ratio must also compare pounds to cost.

The cost of 13 pounds of potatoes is unknown.

To solve the proportion, use the cross products to set up an equation.

$$\frac{5}{\$1.50} \diagup\!\!\!\!\diagdown \frac{13}{n}$$

$$5n = (13)(1.50)$$

Undo multiplication by dividing both sides by 5.

$$\frac{5n}{5} = \frac{19.50}{5}$$

$$n = \$3.90$$

13 pounds of potatoes would cost $3.90.

▶ Write proportions and use cross products to solve. Check your solution.

1. Mandy saved $55 in 5 weeks. At the same rate, how much did she save in 7 weeks?

Proportion ———— unknown amount

a) $\dfrac{\boxed{55}}{\boxed{5}} \begin{array}{l}\text{saved}\\\text{weeks}\end{array} = \dfrac{\boxed{n}}{\boxed{7}} \begin{array}{l}\text{saved}\\\text{weeks}\end{array}$

b) _____
equation

c) _____
solution

Mandy saved $_____ in 7 weeks.

2. You can travel 64 miles on 2 gallons of gasoline. At the same rate, how far can you travel on 9 gallons of gasoline? (First, write the labels on the correct lines.)

Proportion

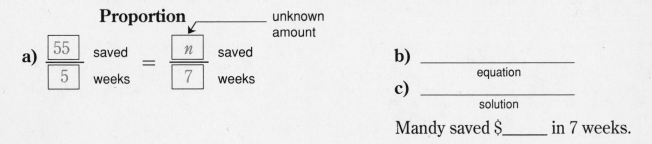

a) $\dfrac{\boxed{}}{\boxed{}} \dfrac{miles}{gallons} = \dfrac{\boxed{}}{\boxed{}} \dfrac{\rule{2cm}{0.4pt}}{\rule{2cm}{0.4pt}}$

b) _____
equation

c) _____
solution

You can travel _____ miles on 9 gallons of gasoline.

Proportions in Problem Solving

▶ Write proportions and use cross products to solve. Check your solution.

1. If 6 pounds of fertilizer covers 6,500 square feet, then 9 pounds of fertilizer will cover how many square feet?

Proportion

a) ⬜ ——— = ⬜ ———
⬜ ——— ⬜ ———

b) _____
equation

c) _____
solution

9 pounds of fertilizer will cover _____.

2. A doughnut recipe calls for 4 eggs for every 48 doughnuts. How many eggs are needed to make 120 doughnuts?

Proportion

a) ⬜ ——— = ⬜ ———
⬜ ——— ⬜ ———

b) _____
equation

c) _____
solution

_____ eggs are needed to make 120 doughnuts.

3. 13 ounces of coffee costs $3.12. At the same rate, what will 20 ounces of coffee cost?

Proportion

a) ⬜ ——— = ⬜ ———
⬜ ——— ⬜ ———

b) _____
equation

c) _____
solution

20 ounces of coffee will cost _____.

4. Amy used 7 gallons of gasoline to travel 196 miles. At this rate, how many gallons will be used on a 532-mile trip?

Proportion

a) ⬜ ——— = ⬜ ———
⬜ ——— ⬜ ———

b) _____
equation

c) _____
solution

_____ gallons will be used on a 532-mile trip.

Mixed Practice

▶ Solve each equation. Check your solution.

1. $m - 17 = 58$

2. $21 = \frac{b}{8}$

3. $71 + s = 229$

4. $7w = 112$

5. $w - 47 = 19$

6. $\frac{n}{4} = 16$

7. For every 2 pounds, roast beef requires a cooking time of 24 minutes. How many minutes are needed to cook a 5-pound roast?

a) $\dfrac{\boxed{}}{\boxed{}}$ $\dfrac{\underline{}}{\underline{}}$ $=$ $\dfrac{\boxed{}}{\boxed{}}$ $\dfrac{\underline{}}{\underline{}}$

b) _____
    equation

c) _____
    solution

8. 1 tablespoon of cocoa mix needs to be added for every 8 ounces of water. How many tablespoons of cocoa are needed for 64 ounces of water?

a) $\dfrac{\boxed{}}{\boxed{}}$ $\dfrac{\underline{}}{\underline{}}$ $=$ $\dfrac{\boxed{}}{\boxed{}}$ $\dfrac{\underline{}}{\underline{}}$

b) _____
    equation

c) _____
    solution

9. Anna's car gets about 26 miles per gallon. About how far could she travel on 12 gallons of gas?

a) $\dfrac{\boxed{}}{\boxed{}}$ $\dfrac{\underline{}}{\underline{}}$ $=$ $\dfrac{\boxed{}}{\boxed{}}$ $\dfrac{\underline{}}{\underline{}}$

b) _____
    equation

c) _____
    solution

Define a Variable

When writing an equation in order to solve a word problem, it is necessary to find the unknown number and assign it a variable (letter). After you have chosen a variable, you have a choice of how to write the equation to solve the problem.

Example

During a two-day business trip, Al traveled 350 miles. He traveled 178 miles by train and the rest by car. How many miles did he travel by car?

Step 1: Find the unknown. $\longrightarrow$ number of miles Al traveled by car
Step 2: Assign a variable. $\longrightarrow$ let m = the number of miles Al traveled by car
Step 3: Write an equation. $\longrightarrow$ $178 + m = 350$ ⎤ Different equations
$m + 178 = 350$ ⎬ can be written for the
$m = 350 - 178$ ⎦ same problem.
Step 4: Solve the equation. $\longrightarrow$ $m = 172$

▶ Find the unknown, assign it a variable, and write two different equations to solve each problem.

1. Andy weighs 185 pounds. He used to weigh 207 pounds. How much weight did Andy lose?

   a) Find the unknown. _____

   b) Assign a variable. _____

   c) Write two equations. _____

                                    _____

   d) Solve the equations. _____

2. Janet had $182.07 in her checking account. She then wrote a check for $43.56. How much money does she have left in her checking account?

   a) Find the unknown. _____

   b) Assign a variable. _____

   c) Write two equations. _____

                                      _____

   d) Solve the equations. _____

Problem-Solving Skills

► For each problem, assign a variable for each unknown. Then write an equation and solve for the unknown.

1. The product of nine and a number is one hundred eight. What is the number?

a) ___let n = the number___
assign a variable

b) _____
equation

c) _____
solution

2. A number minus $33 gives a result of $18. What is the number?

a) _____
assign a variable

b) _____
equation

c) _____
solution

3. A number divided by six gives a result of fifteen. What is the number?

a) _____
assign a variable

b) _____
equation

c) _____
solution

4. JoAnn paid $18 for a dress on sale. It was reduced $15. What was the original price?

a) _____
assign a variable

b) _____
equation

c) _____
solution

5. Roberto worked 32 hours and made a total of $352. How much did he earn per hour?

a) _____
assign a variable

b) _____
equation

c) _____
solution

6. Gregg spent $48 on cassette tapes. Each cassette tape costs $8. How many cassette tapes did he buy?

a) _____
assign a variable

b) _____
equation

c) _____
solution

Two-Step Equations Using a Balance Scale

As you have seen, pictures such as balance scales help us to understand algebra.

Example

The weight of 2 bricks plus 4 one-pound weights equals 10 pounds. Find the weight of 1 brick.

$$2n + 4 = 10$$

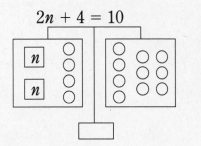

> n = weight of 1 brick
> $2n$ = weight of 2 bricks
> ○ = 1 one-pound weight

Step 1

$$2n + 4 = 10$$

Remove 4 one-pound weights from each side.

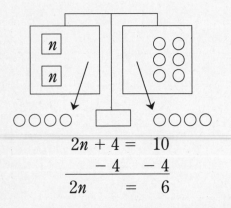

$$
\begin{array}{rcl}
2n + 4 &=& 10 \\
-4 & & -4 \\
\hline
2n &=& 6
\end{array}
$$

Step 2

$$2n = 6$$

To find the weight of 1 brick, divide the bricks and the weights by 2.

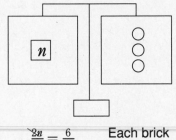

$\dfrac{2n}{2} = \dfrac{6}{2}$ Each brick
$n = 3$ ← weighs 3 pounds.

▶ Use the balance scale to help you solve the problem.

1. The weight of 3 bricks plus 2 one-pound weights equals 8 pounds. Find the weight of 1 brick.

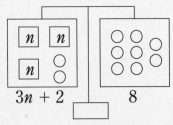

$3n + 2 \qquad 8$

n = weight of 1 brick
$3n$ = weight of 3 bricks

a) Write the equation. _____

b) Remove _____ one-pound weights from each side.

c) Write the new equation. _____

d) Divide the bricks and the weights by _____.

e) The weight of one brick is _____ pounds.

Picture the Equations

▶ Solve each equation by using:
  • boxes to represent variables
  • circles to represent numbers

Equation	Step 1 Draw the picture	Step 2 Get the variables alone	Step 3 Divide
1. $2n + 3 = 13$	 $2n + 3 = 13$	 $2n = 10$	 $n = \underline{\quad 5 \quad}$
2. $5x + 6 = 16$			$x = \underline{\quad\quad}$
3. $\underline{\qquad\qquad}$ write the equation			$n = \underline{\quad\quad}$
4. $4b + 1 = 17$			$b = \underline{\quad\quad}$
5. $3m + 2 = 11$			$m = \underline{\quad\quad}$

Solving Two-Step Equations

Follow this order to solve the two-step equations below:
- First, reverse the addition or subtraction.
- Then, reverse the multiplication by dividing.

Example A

$$2x - 4 = 16 \quad \text{equation}$$
$$\underline{+ 4 \quad + 4} \leftarrow \text{Add: reverse the subtraction.}$$
$$2x \quad = 20$$
$$\frac{2x}{2} \quad = \frac{20}{2} \leftarrow \text{Divide: reverse the multiplication.}$$
$$x \quad = 10 \quad \text{solution}$$

Example B

$$3n + 5 = 11 \quad \text{equation}$$
$$\underline{- 5 \quad - 5} \leftarrow \text{Subtract: reverse the addition.}$$
$$3n \quad = 6$$
$$\frac{3n}{3} \quad = \frac{6}{3} \leftarrow \text{Divide: reverse the multiplication.}$$
$$n \quad = 2 \quad \text{solution}$$

▶ For part a of each question, write what to do first to each side of the equation. For part b, write what to do next to solve the equation. **Do not solve.**

1. $4n + 6 = 18$

   a) First: _Subtract 6 from each side._

   b) Second: _Divide each side by 4._

2. $2t - 5 = 13$

   a) First: _____

   b) Second: _____

3. $8y - 7 = 25$

   a) First: _____

   b) Second: _____

4. $5a + 4 = 19$

   a) First: _____

   b) Second: _____

▶ Solve each equation.

5. $4x + 3 = 15$

6. $6n - 10 = 32$

7. $9x - 8 = 37$

8. $12y + 10 = 70$

More Two-Step Equations

Follow this order in solving the two-step equations below:
- First, reverse the addition or subtraction.
- Then, reverse the division by multiplying.

Example A

$$\frac{a}{5} + 10 = 12 \quad \text{equation}$$
$$\underline{- 10 \quad\quad - 10} \leftarrow \text{Subtract: reverse the addition.}$$
$$\frac{a}{5} \quad\quad = \quad 2$$
$$\cancel{5} \cdot \frac{a}{\cancel{5}} = 2 \cdot 5 \leftarrow \text{Multiply: reverse the division.}$$
$$a = \quad 10 \quad \text{solution}$$

Example B

$$\frac{x}{4} - 2 = \quad 4 \quad \text{equation}$$
$$\underline{+ 2 \quad\quad + 2} \leftarrow \text{Add: reverse the subtraction.}$$
$$\frac{x}{4} \quad\quad = \quad 6$$
$$\cancel{4} \cdot \frac{x}{\cancel{4}} = 6 \cdot 4 \leftarrow \text{Multiply: reverse the division.}$$
$$x = \quad 24 \quad \text{solution}$$

▶ For part a of each question, write what to do first to each side of the equation. For part b, write what to do next to solve the equation. **Do not solve.**

1. $\frac{n}{4} - 1 = 1$

   a) First: _____

   _____

   b) Second: _____

   _____

2. $\frac{x}{2} + 9 = 14$

   a) First: _____

   _____

   b) Second: _____

   _____

3. $\frac{y}{3} - 7 = 10$

   a) First: _____

   _____

   b) Second: _____

   _____

4. $\frac{n}{7} + 3 = 5$

   a) First: _____

   _____

   b) Second: _____

   _____

▶ Solve each equation.

5. $\frac{n}{6} + 4 = 10$

6. $\frac{x}{8} - 5 = 6$

7. $\frac{y}{9} - 3 = 7$

8. $\frac{a}{12} + 8 = 12$

Checking Two-Step Equations

You can check the solution of each equation by replacing the variable in the original equation with the answer.

Example: Check the solution to see whether the answer is correct.

	Step 1	Step 2
	Check by replacing n with 4.	Evaluate
$3n + 2 = 14$ original equation	$\boxed{4}$	$3(4) + 2 = 14$
$n = 4$ solution	$3n + 2 = 14$	$12 + 2 = 14$ $14 = 14$

The solution is correct. $n = 4$

▶ Solve and check the equations.

1. $3n + 15 = 42$ Check:

5. $\frac{x}{2} - 6 = 6$ Check:

2. $5t - 6 = 29$ Check:

6. $7a + 3 = 3$ Check:

3. $\frac{h}{12} - 4 = 7$ Check:

7. $\frac{y}{3} + 9 = 12$ Check:

4. $2n - 9 = 13$ Check:

8. $4m + 19 = 43$ Check:

Translating Word Statements

Define the variable before changing a word statement to an algebraic equation.

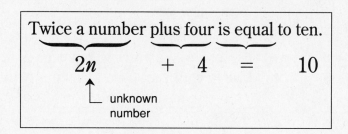

▶ Define the variable and write an equation for each word statement. **Do not solve.**

1. 4 times a number plus 3 is 23.

   a) *let n = a number*
              assign the variable

   b) _____
              equation

2. A number divided by 9, plus 5, is equal to 7.

   a) _____
              assign the variable

   b) _____
              equation

3. 15 more than twice a number is 29.

   a) _____
              assign the variable

   b) _____
              equation

4. 5 is equal to a number divided by 4, minus 10.

   a) _____
              assign the variable

   b) _____
              equation

▶ Match each word statement to the correct equation.

_____ **5.** Eight is equal to a number
letter   divided by two, minus four.

_____ **6.** Four more than twice a number
letter   is eight.

_____ **7.** The difference of twice a number
letter   and four is eight.

_____ **8.** The sum of four and a number
letter   divided by two is eight.

A. $2n + 4 = 8$

B. $\frac{n}{2} + 4 = 8$

C. $2n - 4 = 8$

D. $\frac{n}{2} - 4 = 8$

More Problem Solving

To write an equation based on a word problem, read carefully to find **what** is equal to **what** in the problem. Remember that an equation is balanced around an equal sign.

Example

In a town election, Mr. Hayward received 1,869 votes. This was 36 fewer votes than 5 times the number of votes Mr. Bryant received. How many votes did Mr. Bryant receive?

Assign a variable. v = the number of votes Mr. Bryant received
Write an equation. $1,869 = 5v - 36$
Find the solution. $v = 381$ Mr. Bryant received 381 votes.

You can check your solution by plugging the value you found for v into the equation.

$$1,869 = 5v - 36$$
$$1,869 = 5(381) - 36$$
$$1,869 = 1,905 - 36$$
$$1,869 = 1,869$$

▶ Assign a variable for the unknown value in each problem. Then, write an equation and solve.

1. Alice bought 2 skirts for the same price. She also bought a blouse for $22. If Alice spent a total of $58, what was the price of each skirt?

a) <u> n = price of 1 skirt </u>
       assign a variable

b) _____
       equation

c) _____
       solution

2. Tina bought 5 tires for her car. She paid $240 and received $15 in change. How much did each tire cost?

a) _____
       assign a variable

b) _____
       equation

c) _____
       solution

3. Mike was paid the same wage for 4 weeks. He also received a bonus of $150. If he received a total of $1,250, what were his wages for each week?

a) _____
       assign a variable

b) _____
       equation

c) _____
       solution

4. Martin spent $82 for 3 tickets, including tax. If the tax was $4, how much did each ticket cost?

a) _____
       assign a variable

b) _____
       equation

c) _____
       solution

Review Your Skills

▶ Solve and check each equation. Show your work on another sheet of paper.

1. $t + 24 = 60$

2. $s - 38 = 42$

3. $7m = 91$

4. $3n + 18 = 42$

5. $\frac{a}{4} = 16$

6. $\frac{x}{6} - 8 = 3$

7. $9n - 28 = 26$

8. $\frac{y}{3} + 15 = 21$

▶ Write an equation. Then solve the equation and check your answer.

9. The sum of a number and thirty-eight is one hundred two. What is the number?

   a) _____

   _{equation}

   b) _____

   _{solution}

10. Last week Angie worked 46 hours. If she was paid $414, what was her hourly wage?

    a) _____

    _{equation}

    b) _____

    _{solution}

11. Darrell sold 48 boats. This was 12 more than twice what Mike sold. How many boats did Mike sell?

    a) _____

    _{equation}

    b) _____

    _{solution}

12. If 9 is subtracted from a number divided by 5, the result is 2. What is the number?

    a) _____

    _{equation}

    b) _____

    _{solution}

Negative and Positive Numbers

A thermometer shows equal divisions on both sides of zero.

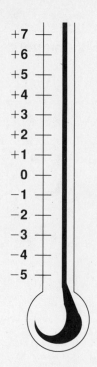

- Numbers less than zero are called **negative** numbers. Negative numbers are always written with a negative sign (−).

- Numbers greater than zero are called **positive** numbers. Positive numbers can be written with a positive sign (+) or with no sign at all.

- Zero on the thermometer separates positive and negative numbers. The number zero is neither positive nor negative.

Words such as *gain, forward, above, increase,* and *up* indicate **positive** (+) values.

Words such as *loss, decrease, down, debt,* and *below* indicate **negative** (−) values.

▶ Write each number with a + (positive) sign or with a − (negative) sign.

1. 7 degrees above zero __+7__

2. 3 degrees below zero _____

3. Positive 5 _____

4. A price increase of $8 _____

5. 20 feet below sea level _____

6. A loss of 4 yards _____

7. A gain of 5 pounds _____

8. Profit of $75 _____

9. 5 steps backwards _____

10. A $15 debt _____

Use the Number Line

All positive and negative numbers and zero are called **integers.** The numbers to the left of zero on the **number line** below are negative integers. The numbers to the right of zero on the number line are positive integers.

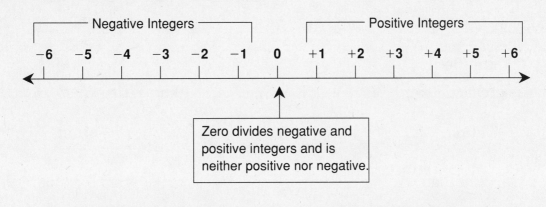

-3 is read as **negative 3.** $+5$ is read as **positive 5.**

▶ Use an integer to show each of the following values.

1. 3 to the right of zero __+3__   **4.** 7 to the right of zero _____

2. 6 to the left of zero _____   **5.** 5 to the right of -6 _____

3. 15 to the left of zero _____   **6.** 8 to the left of $+3$ _____

7. Fill in the integers from -6 to $+3$.
   __-6__ __-5__ _____ _____ _____ _____ _____ _____ __$+3$__

8. Fill in the integers by counting backwards from $+6$ to -4.
   __$+6$__ __$+5$__ _____ _____ _____ _____ _____ _____ _____

9. Count from -6 to $+12$ by twos.
   __-6__ __-4__ _____ _____ _____ _____ _____ _____ __$+12$__

10. Count from -14 to $+10$ by threes.
   __-14__ __-11__ _____ _____ _____ _____ _____ __$+10$__

Comparing and Ordering Integers

You can compare integers using a number line. The greater integer is to the right.

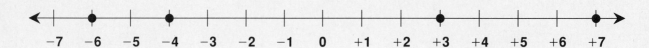

Example A
Which is greater: −4 or −6?

Think:

−4 is to the right of −6,
so −4 is greater than −6.

Example B
Which is smaller: +3 or +7?

Think:

+3 is to the left of +7,
so +3 is smaller than +7.

▶ Place the symbol < (less than) or > (greater than) in the ⬭ to make each statement true.

1. a) +5 ⬭ −3

c) −3 ⬭ −4

e) −8 ⬭ 0

b) +6 ⬭ +12

d) +2 ⬭ −12

f) −4 ⬭ −2

▶ Circle the integer that has the greatest value. Remember that any number written without a sign is always considered positive. Example: +4 can be written as 4.

2. a) 0, −4, −5

c) 8, 0, −1

e) −58, −47, −37

b) −10, −20, −5

d) −5, 2, −1

f) −15, 3, 15

▶ Circle the integer that has the least value.

3. a) −4, 0, 2

c) 9, −1, 15

e) −8, 7, 16

b) −3, −6, −9

d) 13, −13, −12

f) 23, 21, 39

▶ Write the integers in order from smallest to largest.

4. a) 0, −4, 3, −1, 5 _____ _____ _____ _____ _____
smallest   largest

b) 8, −10, 5, −4, 3 _____ _____ _____ _____ _____
smallest   largest

Adding Integers with the Same Sign

It is important to know how to add positive and negative integers. Positive and negative circles will help you discover how to add integers with the same signs.

Example A

Find 4 + 2.

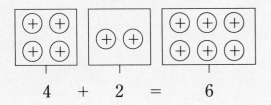

4 + 2 = 6

Example B

Find −3 + (−2).

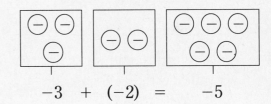

−3 + (−2) = −5

Parentheses are used so the sign of the number is not confused with the operation symbol.

Examples: −3 + (−4) means negative 3 plus negative 4.
              −2 + (−3) means negative 2 plus negative 3.

▶ Complete each number sentence.

1.

<u>−4</u> + <u>(−5)</u> = _____
integer   integer   solution

2.

_____ + _____ = _____
integer   integer   solution

3.

_____ + (_) = _____
integer   integer   solution

▶ Add the integers.

4. −7 + (−3) = _____

5. 9 + 7 = _____

6. −15 + (−10) = _____

7. 13 + 8 = _____

8. −6 + (−4) = _____

9. −16 + (−93) = _____

10. 37 + 95 = _____

Adding Integers with Different Signs

In algebra, we often add integers with different signs.

Example A

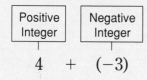

4 + (−3)

Example B

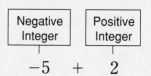

−5 + 2

When the same amount of negatives and positives are combined, they cancel each other out and equal zero.

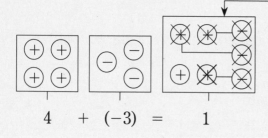

4 + (−3) = 1

The 3 positives and 3 negatives cancel each other out.

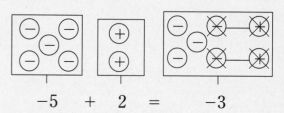

−5 + 2 = −3

▶ Draw positive and negative circles to help solve the problems.

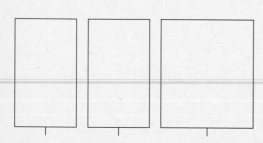

1. 6 + (−4) = _____

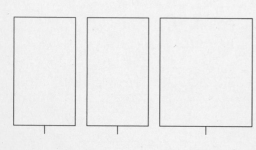

2. −8 + 3 = _____

▶ Add the integers without drawing circles.

3. 7 + (−2) = _____

4. −10 + 4 = _____

5. −3 + 6 = _____

6. 5 + (−8) = _____

7. −14 + 8 = _____

8. 24 + (−15) = _____

9. 31 + (−89) = _____

10. −37 + 95 = _____

Absolute Value

To understand the rules for adding integers, you need to know the meaning of absolute value. The **absolute value** of an integer is its distance from zero.

Example A

−2 and +2 each have an absolute value of 2.
(**Think:** Drop the − or + sign.)

Each has an absolute value of 2.

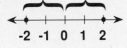

Example B

+8 and −8 each have an absolute value of 8.
(**Think:** Drop the − or + sign.)

Each has an absolute value of 8.

Example C

The absolute value of 0 is 0.

▶ Complete the chart.

1.

Signed Number Value		Absolute Value
a) +5 Drop the + sign. →		5
b) −8 Drop the − sign. →		8
c) +9		
d) −3		
e) −25		
f) +4		

▶ Circle the letter of the number having the greatest absolute value. Think only of the integer without the sign.

2. a) +15   **b)** −6   **c)** +7

3. a) −2   **b)** 0   **c)** +1

4. a) 14   **b)** −18   **c)** −8

5. a) −63   **b)** +18   **c)** +91

▶ Add the absolute values only.

| 7 | | 3 |

6. −7 and +3 _____

7. +8 and −5 _____

8. −9 and −7 _____

9. +14 and +10 _____

▶ Find the difference. Subtract the smaller absolute value from the larger absolute value.

| 5 | | 1 |

10. −5 and +1 _____

11. +4 and −8 _____

12. +36 and −19 _____

13. −27 and +30 _____

Rules for Adding Integers

To add two integers with the **same sign,** you need to
- add their absolute values
- give the answer the common sign

To add two integers with **different signs,** you need to
- find the **difference** of the absolute values
- give the answer the sign of the greater absolute value

Example A

Find $-6 + (-3)$.

absolute values — Drop the negative signs.

| 6 | | 3 |

$-6 \quad + \quad (-3) \quad = \quad -9$

- Add the absolute values: $6 + 3 = 9$
- The common sign is negative, so $(-6) + (-3) = -9$.

Example B

Find $+3 + (-8)$.

absolute values — Drop the + and − signs.

| 3 | | 8 |

$+3 \quad + \quad (-8) \quad = \quad -5$

- Find the difference in absolute values: $8 - 3 = 5$
- The answer is negative because the integer with the greater absolute value is negative, so $3 + (-8) = -5$.

▶ Add the integers.

1. $-18 + 13$

> −18 has a larger absolute value.

  a) Will the answer be + or −? ___−___

  b) _____
    answer

2. $-25 + (-18)$

  a) Will the answer be + or −? _____

  b) _____
    answer

3. $7 + (-15)$

  a) Will the answer be + or −? _____

  b) _____
    answer

4. $-73 + 84$

  a) Will the answer be + or −? _____

  b) _____
    answer

5. $-18 + 27$

> 27 has a larger absolute value.

  a) Will the answer be + or −? _____

  b) _____
    answer

6. $39 + (-14)$

  a) Will the answer be + or −? _____

  b) _____
    answer

7. $-13 + (-55)$

  a) Will the answer be + or −? _____

  b) _____
    answer

8. $192 + 788$

  a) Will the answer be + or −? _____

  b) _____
    answer

Subtracting Integers with the Same Sign

Using positive and negative circles will help you discover how to subtract integers with the same sign.

Example A

Find $5 - (+3)$.

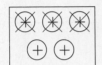

Take away 3 of the 5 circles. 2 are left, and they're positive.
$5 - (+3) = 2$

Example B

Find $-6 - (-5)$.

Take away 5 of the 6 circles. 1 is left, and it's negative.
$-6 - (-5) = -1$

▶ Draw positive and negative circles to help solve the problems.

1.

$-4 - (-2) = $ _____

2.

$8 - (+2) = $ _____

3.

$-7 - (-4) = $ _____

▶ Subtract the integers without drawing circles.

4. $-6 - (-2) = $ _____

5. $12 - (+7) = $ _____

6. $-35 - (-12) = $ _____

7. $28 - (+16) = $ _____

8. $-529 - (-345) = $ _____

9. $-197 - (-58) = $ _____

10. $1,205 - (+384) = $ _____

Relating Subtraction to Addition

Using positive and negative circles will help you to discover how subtraction relates to addition. Compare the addition and subtraction sentences.

Example

Find $4 - (+2)$.

$4 - (+2) = 2$

Find $4 + (-2)$.

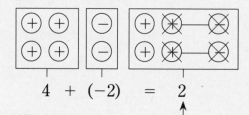

$4 + (-2) = 2$

same answers

The result of subtracting $+2$ is the same as adding -2.

▶ Use positive and negative circles to help solve the problems.

1. a) $-5 - (-3) =$ _____ **b)** $-5 + (+3) =$ _____

 c) The result of subtracting -3 is the same as adding what integer? _____

2. a) $-6 - (-2) =$ _____ **b)** $-6 + (+2) =$ _____

 c) The result of subtracting _____ is the same as adding $+2$.
 <u>integer</u>

 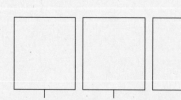

3. a) $-5 - (-4) =$ _____ **b)** $-5 + (+4) =$ _____

 c) The result of subtracting _____ is the same as adding _____ .
 <u>integer</u>   <u>integer</u>

Using Opposites

▶ Use positive and negative numbers to write the opposites.

1. A gain of 4 yards __+4__

2. A loss of 4 yards __−4__

3. 7 degrees below zero _____

4. 7 degrees above zero _____

5. 30 feet above sea level _____

6. 30 feet below sea level _____

7. Positive 5 _____

8. Negative 5 _____

9. Write the opposite of each integer.

a) −8 _____
      opposite

b) +7 _____
      opposite

c) −15 _____
       opposite

d) 5 _____
   opposite

When subtracting integers:
- Rewrite the subtraction problem as an addition problem.
- Change the number you are subtracting to its opposite.

$$\text{change to addition}$$

Example: $6 - (+4) = 6 + (-4)$

$$\text{opposites}$$

▶ Use addition to rewrite each problem. **Do not solve.**

change to addition

10. $-5 - (-3) = -5 \;\square\; \underline{}$
         symbol
       opposites

13. $-8 - (+22)$

11. $-8 - (+9)$

14. $35 - (-13)$

12. $11 - (-7)$

15. $+47 - (+15)$

Rules for Subtracting Integers

To subtract one integer from another, you need to
- change the subtraction sign to an addition sign
- change the sign of the number being subtracted
- add the integers

Subtracting an integer	is the same as ▶	Adding its opposite

Example: Find $-3 - (+8)$.

change to addition

$$-3 - (+8) = -3 + (-8) = -11$$

opposites

▶ Subtract the integers.

1. $9 - (+4)$

$$\underline{\ \ 9\ \ } \boxed{+} \underline{(-4)} = \underline{\ \ \ \ }$$
To subtract 4, add −4.

2. $-7 - (-2)$

$$\underline{\ \ \ \ } \boxed{+} \underline{\ \ \ \ } = \underline{\ \ \ \ }$$
symbol

3. $8 - (-10)$

$$\underline{\ \ \ \ } \boxed{\ } \underline{\ \ \ \ } = \underline{\ \ \ \ }$$
symbol

4. $3 - (+20)$

$$\underline{\ \ \ \ } \boxed{\ } \underline{\ \ \ \ } = \underline{\ \ \ \ }$$
symbol

5. $-11 - (+2)$

$$\underline{-11} \boxed{\ } \underline{\ \ \ \ } = \underline{\ \ \ \ }$$
symbol

6. $-19 - (-5)$

$$\underline{-19} \boxed{+} \underline{(+5)} = \underline{\ \ \ \ }$$
To subtract (−5), add 5.

7. $56 - (-13)$

$$\underline{\ \ \ \ } \boxed{+} \underline{\ \ \ \ } = \underline{\ \ \ \ }$$
symbol

8. $27 - (+52)$

$$\underline{\ \ \ \ } \boxed{\ } \underline{\ \ \ \ } = \underline{\ \ \ \ }$$
symbol

9. $14 - (+6)$

$$\underline{\ \ \ \ } \boxed{\ } \underline{\ \ \ \ } = \underline{\ \ \ \ }$$
symbol

10. $195 - (-459)$

$$\underline{\ \ \ \ } \boxed{\ } \underline{\ \ \ \ } = \underline{\ \ \ \ }$$
symbol

Adding and Subtracting Integers

▶ Change all subtraction problems to addition problems first. Then add the integers.

1. $12 + (-5) =$ _____

$\boxed{9 + 15}$
2. $9 - (-15) =$ _____

$\boxed{14 + (-20)}$
3. $14 - (+20) =$ _____

4. $-15 + (-30) =$ _____

5. $-45 + 56 =$ _____

$\boxed{8 + 3}$
6. $8 - (-3) =$ _____

7. $18 + 45 =$ _____

8. $-5 - (+12) =$ _____

9. $-3 - (-15) =$ _____

10. $-28 + 12 =$ _____

11. $81 - (-33) =$ _____

12. $203 + (-203) =$ _____

13. $93 + 74 =$ _____

14. $32 - (+45) =$ _____

15. $-145 - (+816) =$ _____

16. $-345 + (-156) =$ _____

Applications Using Integers

▶ Integers are often used in real life. Solve the problems below.

Problem	Sentence	Solution
1. During the day the temperature rose 12 degrees from 4 degrees below 0. What was the temperature after it rose 12 degrees?	$-4 + 12 =$ _____	The temperature was _____ degrees.
2. What is the temperature when 45° is followed by a drop of 16°?	$45 + (-16) =$ _____	The temperature is _____°.
3. The Badgers football team gained 9 yards on the first play. On the next play there was a loss of 4 yards. What were the total yards gained or lost?	$9 + (-4) =$ _____	_____ yards were _____. gained or lost

▶ Complete each sentence and solve.

Problem	Sentence	Solution
4. A diver descended 16 feet below sea level the first minute and 24 feet the second minute. How many feet is this below sea level?	_____ _____ _____ = _____ integer · operation sign · integer	absolute value ⌐ The diver is _____ feet below sea level.
5. Mary had $69 in her checking account. She wrote a check for $75. What amount will her checking account show now?	_____ _____ _____ = _____ integer · operation sign · integer	_____ is the balance of her checking account.

Multiplying Integers with Different Signs

You do not need the multiplication symbol ($\times$) when multiplying integers.
$(-2)(3)$ means negative 2 times positive 3.

> To multiply two numbers with **different** signs, multiply their absolute values. The answer is **negative.** Multiplying a negative integer by a positive integer results in a negative integer.

Multiply.

Example: Find $(-2)(3)$.

Step 1

Multiply the absolute values.

$2 \times 3 = 6$

Step 2

Give the answer a negative sign.

$(-2)(3) = -6$

The order of the numbers being multiplied does not affect your answer.

$(4)(-3)$ is the same as $(-3)(4)$.

$$(4)(-3) = -12 \qquad (-3)(4) = -12$$

same result

▶ Multiply the integers in each problem.

1. $(-5)(8) = \underline{-40}$

5. $(25)(-15) = \underline{}$

2. $(4)(-12) = \underline{}$

6. $(-44)(3) = \underline{}$

3. $(15)(-3) = \underline{}$

7. $(31)(-41) = \underline{}$

4. $(-10)(7) = \underline{}$

8. $(-8)(630) = \underline{}$

Multiplying Integers with the Same Sign

> When multiplying two numbers with the **same** signs, multiply their absolute values. The answer is **positive.**

Example A
Find $(-5)(-8)$.

- Multiply their absolute values.

$$5 \times 8 = 40$$

- The answer is **positive.**

$$(-5)(-8) = +40$$

Example B
Find $(+6)(+3)$.

- Multiply their absolute values.

$$6 \times 3 = 18$$

- The answer is **positive.**

$$(+6)(+3) = +18$$

Remember: Positive numbers can be written with a positive sign $(+)$ or with no sign at all.

▶ Multiply the integers to find each answer.

1. $(-5)(-15) = $ _____

2. $(7)(12) = $ _____

3. $(39)(6) = $ _____

4. $(-84)(-21) = $ _____

5. $(3)(42) = $ _____

6. $(-10)(-10) = $ _____

7. $(-25)(-5) = $ _____

8. $(4)(11) = $ _____

9. $(12)(5) = $ _____

10. $(-7)(-9) = $ _____

11. $(7)(3) = $ _____

12. $(-64)(-12) = $ _____

13. $(-4)(-19) = $ _____

14. $(8)(9) = $ _____

15. $(-125)(-3) = $ _____

16. $(22)(5) = $ _____

17. $(-48)(-2) = $ _____

18. $(-35)(-10) = $ _____

19. $(20)(50) = $ _____

20. $(-57)(-100) = $ _____

Multiplying Integers

▶ Complete each sentence with the word positive or negative.

1. A negative integer times a positive integer is a _____ integer.
<u>positive or negative</u>

2. A positive integer times a positive integer is a _____ integer.
<u>positive or negative</u>

3. A positive integer times a negative integer is a _____ integer.
<u>positive or negative</u>

4. A negative integer times a negative integer is a _____ integer.
<u>positive or negative</u>

───

▶ Multiply the integers.

5. $(-11)(7)$
   a) Will the answer be + or −? _____
   b) _____
      <u>answer</u>

6. $(-5)(-9)$
   a) Will the answer be + or −? _____
   b) _____
      <u>answer</u>

7. $(10)(6)$
   a) Will the answer be + or −? _____
   b) _____
      <u>answer</u>

8. $(4)(-12)$
   a) Will the answer be + or −? _____
   b) _____
      <u>answer</u>

9. $(-8)(3)$
   a) Will the answer be + or −? _____
   b) _____
      <u>answer</u>

10. $(-59)(-9)$
   a) Will the answer be + or −? _____
   b) _____
      <u>answer</u>

11. $(-28)(25)$
   a) Will the answer be + or −? _____
   b) _____
      <u>answer</u>

12. $(-4)(-205)$
   a) Will the answer be + or −? _____
   b) _____
      <u>answer</u>

13. $(24)(15)$
   a) Will the answer be + or −? _____
   b) _____
      <u>answer</u>

14. $(-9)(861)$
   a) Will the answer be + or −? _____
   b) _____
      <u>answer</u>

Dividing Integers with Different Signs

You have already worked with forms of algebra relating multiplication and division equations. Multiplication and division are inverse operations.

▶ Complete the chart.

	Multiplication Equation	Division Equation	Rule
1. a)	$(-5)(-7) = +35$	$(+35) \div (-7) = \underline{-5}$	$(+) \div (-) = \underline{\quad}$ sign
b)	$(-6)(+4) = -24$	$(-24) \div (+4) = \underline{\quad}$	$(-) \div (+) = \underline{\quad}$ sign
c)	$(-8)(+9) = -72$	$(-72) \div (+9) = \underline{\quad}$	$(-) \div (+) = \underline{\quad}$ sign
d)	$(-3)(-2) = +6$	$(+6) \div (-3) = \underline{\quad}$	$(+) \div (-) = \underline{\quad}$ sign

> To divide two numbers with **different** signs, divide their absolute values. The answer is **negative.**

Example A

Find $(-36) \div (+9)$.
- Divide the absolute values.
  $$36 \div 9 = 4$$
- The answer is negative.
  $$(-36) \div (+9) = -4$$

Example B

Find $(+56) \div (-8)$.
- Divide the absolute values.
  $$56 \div 8 = 7$$
- The answer is negative.
  $$(+56) \div (-8) = -7$$

▶ Divide the integers.

2. $(-24) \div (+6) = \underline{\quad}$

3. $72 \div (-2) = \underline{\quad}$

4. $135 \div (-15) = \underline{\quad}$

5. $(-81) \div 9 = \underline{\quad}$

6. $91 \div (-13) = \underline{\quad}$

7. $(-30) \div 10 = \underline{\quad}$

8. $(-45) \div 5 = \underline{\quad}$

9. $77 \div (-7) = \underline{\quad}$

Dividing Integers with the Same Sign

Division equations are based on multiplication equations.

▶ Complete the chart.

	Multiplication Equation	Division Equation	Rule
1. a)	$(+3)(+4) = +12$	$(+12) \div (+4) = \underline{3}$	$(+) \div (+) = \underline{+}$ sign
b)	$(+4)(-5) = -20$	$(-20) \div (-5) = \underline{}$	$(-) \div (-) = \underline{}$ sign
c)	$(-5)(+9) = -45$	$(-45) \div (-5) = \underline{}$	$(-) \div (-) = \underline{}$ sign
d)	$(+8)(+7) = +56$	$(+56) \div (+7) = \underline{}$	$(+) \div (+) = \underline{}$ sign

> To divide two numbers with the **same** sign, divide their absolute values. The answer is **positive.**

Example A

Find $(-40) \div (-4)$.
- Divide the absolute values.
$$40 \div 4 = 10$$
- The answer can be written with a positive sign or no sign.
$$(-40) \div (-4) = +10$$

Example B

Find $(+24) \div (+6)$.
- Divide the absolute values.
$$24 \div 6 = 4$$
- The answer is positive.
$$(+24) \div (+6) = +4$$

▶ Divide the integers.

2. $(-63) \div (-7) = \underline{}$

3. $50 \div 10 = \underline{}$

4. $(-76) \div (-19) = \underline{}$

5. $(-84) \div (-6) = \underline{}$

6. $185 \div 37 = \underline{}$

7. $(-260) \div (-4) = \underline{}$

8. $(-161) \div (-23) = \underline{}$

9. $156 \div (+12) = \underline{}$

Dividing Integers

► Complete each sentence with the word positive or negative.

1. A negative number divided by a negative number is a _____ number.
positive or negative

2. A positive number divided by a positive number is a _____ number.
positive or negative

3. A positive number divided by a negative number is a _____ number.
positive or negative

4. A negative number divided by a positive number is a _____ number.
positive or negative

_____

► Decide whether the answer will be positive or negative. Then divide the integers.

5. $15 \div (-5)$

   a) Will the answer be + or −? _____

   b) _____
      answer

6. $\dfrac{-54}{9}$

   a) Will the answer be + or −? _____

   b) _____
      answer

7. $21 \div 3$

   a) Will the answer be + or −? _____

   b) _____
      answer

8. $\dfrac{-42}{-6}$

   a) Will the answer be + or −? _____

   b) _____
      answer

9. $-16 \div 4$

   a) Will the answer be + or −? _____

   b) _____
      answer

10. $(-204) \div (-6)$

   a) Will the answer be + or −? _____

   b) _____
      answer

11. $180 \div (-12)$

   a) Will the answer be + or −? _____

   b) _____
      answer

12. $306 \div 17$

   a) Will the answer be + or −? _____

   b) _____
      answer

13. $(-300) \div (-20)$

   a) Will the answer be + or −? _____

   b) _____
      answer

14. $(-376) \div 47$

   a) Will the answer be + or −? _____

   b) _____
      answer

Review of Integers

▶ Solve the following problems.

1. 15 (−35) = _____

2. −97 − (−48) = _____

3. 41 + (−63) = _____

4. −75 ÷ 15 = _____

5. −23 + (−19) = _____

6. (−8) (−22) = _____

7. (−217) ÷ (−7) = _____

8. 51 − 70 = _____

▶ Write < (less than) or > (greater than) to make each statement true.

9. (+15) (−4) (<) 5(12)
   −60   60

10. 12 + (−5) ( ) −12 + (−5)

11. −32 ÷ (−4) ( ) 54 ÷ (−3)

12. 28 − (−12) ( ) 75 − (+36)

13. −63 + 19 ( ) 28 + 17

14. 50 ÷ (−2) ( ) 75 ÷ 5

15. −30 − (+4) ( ) −20 − (−14)

16. −12 (4) ( ) (−11) (−7)

Applications Using Integers

Sometimes, in real life, we use integers to multiply and divide.

▶ Complete each sentence and solve using integers. Then write each answer as an absolute value.

Problem	Sentence	Solution

1. The temperature dropped 5 degrees each hour from 1:00 A.M. to 5:00 A.M. What was the drop in temperature?

$$\underset{\text{integer}}{-5°} \quad \underset{\substack{\text{operation}\\\text{symbol}}}{\times} \quad \underset{\text{integer}}{4\text{ hrs.}} = -20°$$

means the same as a negative number

The drop in temperature was __20__ degrees.

↑ absolute value

2. A diver descended 64 feet below sea level in 4 minutes. On the average, how many feet did he descend each minute?

$$\underset{\text{integer}}{\underline{\hspace{2em}}} \quad \underset{\substack{\text{operation}\\\text{symbol}}}{\underline{\hspace{2em}}} \quad \underset{\text{integer}}{\underline{\hspace{2em}}} = \underline{\hspace{2em}}$$

The diver descended _____ feet on the average each minute.

3. 5 buses took a total of 315 students to a basketball game. If there were an equal number of students per bus, how many students were on each bus?

$$\underset{\text{integer}}{\underline{\hspace{2em}}} \quad \underset{\substack{\text{operation}\\\text{symbol}}}{\underline{\hspace{2em}}} \quad \underset{\text{integer}}{\underline{\hspace{2em}}} = \underline{\hspace{2em}}$$

_____ students on each bus.

4. Jerry is $425 in debt. Bill owes 5 times that amount. How much does Bill owe?

$$\underset{\text{integer}}{\underline{\hspace{2em}}} \quad \underset{\substack{\text{operation}\\\text{symbol}}}{\underline{\hspace{2em}}} \quad \underset{\text{integer}}{\underline{\hspace{2em}}} = \underline{\hspace{2em}}$$

Bill owes _____.

5. If a train travels at a rate of 45 mph, how far will it travel in 8 hours?

$$\underset{\text{integer}}{\underline{\hspace{2em}}} \quad \underset{\substack{\text{operation}\\\text{symbol}}}{\underline{\hspace{2em}}} \quad \underset{\text{integer}}{\underline{\hspace{2em}}} = \underline{\hspace{2em}}$$

The train will travel _____ miles.

Multistep Problems Using Integers

▶ Use the answer you find in the first part of each question to help you answer the second part of each question.

1. a) A diver needs to descend to a depth of 128 feet below sea level to reach the bottom. He can descend 16 feet each minute. How many minutes will it take to reach the bottom?

___8___

b) The diver's air tank will hold enough air for 45 minutes. It takes him as much time to reach the surface as it did to get to the bottom. How many minutes can he stay on the bottom?

_____

2. a) Gwen owed $1,215 on her charge card. During the next four months she made equal payments of $225 each month. How much did she pay?

_____

b) How much does she have left to pay on her charge card?

_____

3. a) Chris had $875 in her savings account. The first week she withdrew $490. How much money was left in her savings account?

_____

b) The next week she made a deposit of $326. How much money does she now have in her savings account?

_____

4. a) At 6:00 P.M. the temperature was 17°. The temperature dropped at a rate of 4° every hour for 6 hours. How many degrees did the temperature drop?

_____

b) What was the temperature at midnight?

_____

5. a) Wooten Tool & Die had a profit of $4,580 the first month. The second month it lost $9,450. What were the company's earnings over the two months?

_____

b) After three months Wooten Tool & Die showed a profit of $2,460. How much did the company make in the third month?

_____

Learning Order of Operations

Two or more numbers combined is called an **expression.** Expressions may need to be simplified. When simplifying an expression, work from left to right.

Example A

Find $(-3)(2)(-1)$.

$(-3)(2)(-1)$ ← Multiply (-3) and (2).

$(-6)\ (-1)$ ← Multiply (-6) and (-1).

6 ← The answer is 6.

Example B

Find $5 + (-3) - (-8)$.

| Remember: Add +8. |

$5 + (-3) - (-8)$ ← Add 5 and (-3).

$2\ \ +\ \ 8$ ← Add 2 and 8.

10 ← The answer is 10.

▶ Simplify each expression.

1. $(-8)(-5)(2)$

$(\ \underline{40}\ )(\ \underline{2}\ )$

_____

| Add +7. |

2. $28 - (-7) + 8$

_____ + _____

_____

3. $(-6)(-4)(-2)$

$(\underline{\ \ \ \ })(\underline{\ \ \ \ })$

_____

| Add (−6). |

4. $13 + (-10) - 6 = $ _____

5. $(9)(-6)(7) = $ _____

6. $-36 \div 6 \div 2 = $ _____

| Add +25. | | Add +15. |

7. $50 - (-25) - (-15) = $ _____

| Add (−4). |

8. $-15 + 8 - 4 = $ _____

| Add +7. | | Add (−9). |

9. $28 - (-7) + 5 - 9 = $ _____

10. $(2)(-4)(6)(5) = $ _____

Ordering Expressions

To simplify the expression $4 + 6(2)$, would your answer be 20 or 16?

The correct value is 16, because multiplication (6 times 2) must be done before addition. To make sure all expressions have only one value, a specific order of operations must be followed.

> **Multiply and divide from left to right before adding and subtracting from left to right.**

Example A

Find $(-6) + 2\,(-4)$.

$(-6) + 2\,(-4)$ ← Multiply 2 by (-4).

$(-6) + (-8)$ ← Add (-6) and (-8).

-14 ⟵ The answer is -14.

Example B

Find $-14 + 24 \div 2$.

$-14 + 24 \div 2$ ← Divide 24 by 2.

$-14 + 12$ ← Add -14 and 12.

-2 ⟵ The answer is -2.

▶ Simplify each expression.

1. $5\,(-4) + 9$

_____ $+ 9 =$ _____

2. $-4 + (6)\,(5)$

$-4 +$ _____ $=$ _____

3. $17 + 10 \div 2$

$17 +$ _____ $=$ _____

4. $12 - (3)\,(-2) + 9$

$12 -$ _____ $+ 9 =$ _____

5. $46 - 30 \div 5 =$ _____

6. $7(4) + 9 - (-2) =$ _____

7. $45 - 9 + (3)\,(5) =$ _____

8. $16 \div 4 + (7)\,(3) =$ _____

9. $5 + 9 - 6 + 8 =$ _____

10. $36 \div 6 \div (-3) =$ _____

Simplify the Expression

When working with expressions that include **grouping symbols** ( ) or [ ], always simplify inside the grouping symbols first.

Order of Operation Rules
First: Do all operations inside the grouping symbols.
Second: **Multiply** or **divide** from left to right.
Third: **Add** or **subtract** from left to right.

Example: Find $5(2 + 4) - 6$.

$5(2 + 4) - 6$ ← Do the work inside the grouping symbols $(2 + 4)$.

$5(6) \quad - 6$ ← Multiply 5 times (6).

$30 \quad - 6$ ← Subtract 6.

24 ← The answer is 24.

▶ Simplify each expression.

1. $3(-2) - (3 + 1)$ Add within ( ).

$3(-2) -$ _____ Multiply.

_____ $-$ _____ $=$ _____

2. $25 - 3(5 - 3)$

$25 - 3($ _____ $)$

$25 -$ _____ $=$ _____

3. $5[9 + (-15) - 3]$

$5($ _____ $) =$ _____

4. $3[8 + (-3)] - 21 =$ _____

5. $15 - 4(3 + 2) =$ _____

6. $(6 + 4)3 =$ _____

7. $2(7 + 5) \div 2 =$ _____

8. $(-5)[(-3) - (-2)] =$ _____

9. $15 - (2 + 6)3 =$ _____

10. $4(-3) + 8[4 + (-2)] =$ _____

Using Order of Operation

▶ Circle the letter of the operation to be done first.

1. $7 + 6 - 10$ **a)** addition   **b)** subtraction

2. $18 - 9 \div (3)(2)$ **a)** subtraction   **b)** division   **c)** multiplication

3. $25 - (2+16) \div 3$ **a)** subtraction   **b)** addition   **c)** division

4. $6(4) \div 2$ **a)** multiplication   **b)** division

▶ Circle the letter of the correct answer for each expression.

5. $3 + 5(2) - 7$ **a)** 9   **b)** -22 **c)** 6

6. $6(-2) + 5(-2) + 6$ **a)** -16 **b)** -28 **c)** 8

7. $3(6) - 4 \div 2$ **a)** 3   **b)** 16   **c)** 7

8. $[6 + (-4)]3$ **a)** -6 **b)** 6   **c)** 30

▶ Insert the grouping symbols to make each sentence true.

9. $3 + 9 \div 3 - 1 = 6$ **11.** $7 + 2 \times 3 + 4 = 31$

10. $3 \times 6 + 4 \div 2 = 15$ **12.** $30 \div 6 + 4 \times 5 = 15$

▶ Fill in each ☐ with $+$, $-$, $\times$, or $\div$ to make each sentence true.

13. $12 \;\square\; 7 \;\square\; 3 = 16$ **15.** $-15 \;\square\; 5 \;\square\; (-4) = -7$

14. $(6 \;\square\; 4) \;\square\; 3 = 30$ **16.** $30 \;\square\; 4 \;\square\; (8 \;\square\; 2) = 6$

Exponents

In algebra, we sometimes work with **exponents.**

Exponent: the number of times 2 is used as a factor

2^3 → 2 to the third power

Base: the number used as a factor

3 factors

2^3 means (2) (2) (2)

4   (2)

8

Some expressions may have a negative number as a base. In such cases, remember the rules for multiplying integers.

$(-2)^2 = (-2)\,(-2) = +4$ A negative times a negative equals a positive.

$(-2)^3 = (-2)\,(-2)\,(-2)$

+4 (-2) A negative times a positive equals a negative.

-8

▶ Complete the chart.

	Expression	Base	Exponent	Meaning	Value
1.	3^2	3	2	(3) (3)	9
2.	$(-2)^5$				
3.		5	4		
4.	2^6				
5.				$(-4)\,(-4)\,(-4)\,(-4)$	
6.	$(-3)^3$				
7.		10	3		

▶ Fill in the values for each ☐.

8. $3^{\square} = 27$

9. $5^{\square} = 25$

10. $2^{\square} = 16$

11. $\square^2 = 4$

12. $\square^2 = 9$

13. $\square^3 = 125$

Evaluate Expressions

You can **evaluate** (find the value of) an algebraic expression when you know the value of each variable:
- First, replace each variable with its value.
- Then perform the indicated operation.

Example A

Evaluate $n + 3$ if $n = 5$.

$\boxed{5}$

$n + 3$ ← Replace n with 5.

$5 + 3$ ← Add 5 + 3.

8 ← The answer is 8.

Example B

Evaluate $3y$ if $y = (-2)$.

$\boxed{-2}$

$3y$ ← Replace y with (-2).

$3(-2)$ ← Multiply 3 by (-2).

-6 ← The answer is -6.

▶ Evaluate each expression if $a = (-2)$, $b = 3$, and $c = 1$.

1. $15 + b$ ← Replace b with 3.

$15 +$ _____ ← Add.

_____
answer

2. $20 \div a$ ← Replace a with (-2).

$20 \div$ _____ ← Divide.

_____
answer

$\boxed{5 \text{ times } c}$

3. $5c + a$ ← Replace c with 1 and a with (-2).

$5($ _____ $) + ($ _____ $)$ ← Multiply.

_____ $+ (-2)$ ← Add.

_____
answer

$\boxed{a \text{ times } b}$

4. $ab + c =$ _____

5. $(-3) + a =$ _____

$\boxed{a \text{ times } b \text{ times } c}$

6. $abc =$ _____

7. $a + b + c =$ _____

8. $ab - 3c =$ _____

9. $2a + 3b =$ _____

$\boxed{2b \text{ divided by } a}$

10. $\frac{2b}{a} =$ _____

Evaluate with Exponents

Sometimes an algebraic expression has exponents. When evaluating exponents, write the meaning of each exponent. Think: $n^3 = (n)(n)(n)$.

Example A

Evaluate $4n + n^3$ if $n = 2$.

$\boxed{(n)(n)(n)}$

$4n + n^3$ ← Replace n with 2.

$4(2) + (2)(2)(2)$ ← Multiply.

$8 + 8$ ← Add.

16 ← The answer is 16.

Example B

Evaluate $2a + b^3$ if $a = 5$ and $b = (-3)$.

$\boxed{(b)(b)(b)}$

$2a + b^3$ ← Replace a and b.

$2(5) + (-3)(-3)(-3)$ ← Multiply.

$10 + (-27)$ ← Add.

-17 ← The answer is -17.

▶ Evaluate if $a = 2$, $b = 3$, and $c = (-2)$.

1. $\boxed{(b)(b)}$

$4a + b^2$ ← Replace a and b.

$4(\underline{\ 2\ }) + (\underline{\ 3\ })(\underline{\ 3\ })$ ← Multiply.

$\underline{\hspace{2cm}} + \underline{\hspace{2cm}}$ ← Add.

$\overline{\text{answer}}$

2. $\boxed{(c)(c)(c)}$

$5c^3$ ← Replace c.

$5(\underline{\hspace{1.5cm}})(\underline{\hspace{1.5cm}})(\underline{\hspace{1.5cm}})$ ← Multiply.

$\overline{\text{answer}}$

3. $\boxed{(b)(b)}$ $\boxed{(c)(c)(c)}$

$b^2 - c^3$ ← Replace b and c.

$(\underline{\hspace{1cm}})(\underline{\hspace{1cm}}) - (\underline{\hspace{1cm}})(\underline{\hspace{1cm}})(\underline{\hspace{1cm}})$ ← Multiply.

$\underline{\hspace{2cm}} - \underline{\hspace{2cm}}$ ← Add the opposite.

$\overline{\text{answer}}$

4. $a^4 + bc =$ _____

5. $3a^2 + b =$ _____

6. $b^2 - c =$ _____

$\boxed{a \times b^2 \times c}$

7. $ab^2 c =$ _____

8. $c^3 - a =$ _____

9. $a + b^2 + c =$ _____

10. $18 - c^2 =$ _____

Review Your Skills

▶ Simplify each expression.

	Expression	Answer
1.	$15 - 16 \div 4$	
2.	$(4)(-2) + 5$	
3.	$-6 + (5)(6) \div 3$	
4.	$9(-4) - (10 - 7)$	
5.	$7 - 9 + 2 - 5$	
6.	$4[7 + (-12) - 4]$	
7.	$7[(-4) - (-5)]$	
8.	$7(-9) + 4[8 + (-15)]$	

▶ Fill in each ☐ with $+$, $-$, $\times$, or $\div$ to make each sentence true.

9. $3\,☐\,5\,☐\,9 = 24$

10. $(17\,☐\,3)\,☐\,(-5) = -4$

11. $13\,☐\,7\,☐\,(-1) = 5$

▶ Fill in the values for each ☐.

12. $4^2 = ☐$

13. $☐^3 = 8$

14. $(-3)^4 = ☐$

▶ Choose a variable and write an algebraic expression for each word expression.

15. Fifteen more than a number

_____

16. The product of nine and a number

_____

17. Thirty-five decreased by a number

_____

18. A number divided by six

_____

▶ Evaluate the algebraic expressions if $a = 2$, $b = (-3)$, and $c = 4$.

19. $5a + b = $ _____

20. $ac - b = $ _____

21. $\frac{2bc}{a} = $ _____

22. $a^3 - b + 4 = $ _____

23. $a^2 + b^2 + c^3 = $ _____

24. $\frac{9c}{b} + 3a = $ _____

Learning about Formulas

A **formula** is a set of mathematical instructions that is written as an equation. Formulas have been developed to make working with math easier and faster.

The following formula describes how to find the distance traveled. More than one variable (letter) can be used in the equation.

The **distance** traveled is equal to the **rate of speed** multiplied by the **time.**

$$D \qquad = \qquad r \qquad \cdot \qquad t$$

written as
$D = rt$

▶ Change each sentence to a formula.

1. Interest (I) is equal to the principal (p) times the rate (r) times the time (t).

_____
formula

2. The time (T) to cook a turkey is equal to 20 minutes times the weight (w).

_____
formula

3. The total cost (C) of one item is equal to the price (p) plus the tax (t).

_____
formula

4. The area (A) of a rectangle is equal to the length (l) times the width (w).

_____
formula

_____

▶ Write out what each formula means.

5. $C = np$ when C = the total cost, n = the number of units bought, and p = the price for one unit _The total cost equals the number of units_ _times the price for one unit._

6. $A = \frac{1}{2}bh$ when A = area of a triangle, b = the length of the base, and h = the height of the triangle _____

_____

7. $P = 4s$ when P = perimeter of a square and s = length of one side

_____

8. $P = 100 - 5n$ when P = percent score of a 20-point quiz and n = number of wrong answers _____

_____

Using Formulas

When using a formula, replace the variables with the values that are given.

Example: How many miles did Marsha travel if she drove 55 mph for 3 hours?

Step 1

The distance traveled (D) is equal to the rate of speed (r) multiplied by the time (t).

$$D = r\,t$$

formula

Step 2

Replace the variables with the values you know.

55 3

$$D = r\,t$$

Step 3

Solve to find the distance traveled.

$$D = (55)(3)$$
$$D = 165$$

Marsha traveled 165 miles.

▶ Use the formula $T = 35w$ to find the time needed to roast a pork loin whose weight is given. T = time needed to roast a pork loin, and w = weight of pork loin.

1. How many minutes would it take to roast a 10-pound pork loin?

10

$$T = 35w$$
$$T = \text{\_\_\_\_\_ minutes}$$

2. How many minutes would it take to roast a 16-pound pork loin?

$$T = 35w$$
$$T = \text{\_\_\_\_\_ minutes}$$

▶ Use the tax table and the formula $C = np + t$ to find the total cost. C = total cost, n = number of units, p = price for one unit, and t = tax.

3. What is the total cost for 3 pairs of socks?

$$C = np + t$$
$$C = \$ \text{_____}$$

$1.79

Sales Tax Table	
Amount	**Tax**
$3.92 to $4.08	$.24
4.09 to 4.24	.25
4.25 to 4.41	.26
4.42 to 4.58	.27
4.59 to 4.74	.28
4.75 to 4.91	.29
4.92 to 5.08	.30
5.09 to 5.24	.31
5.25 to 5.41	.32
5.42 to 5.58	.33
5.59 to 5.74	.34
5.75 to 5.91	.35

4. What is the total cost for 2 boxes of greeting cards?

$$C = np + t$$
$$C = \$ \text{_____}$$

$2.89

Simple Interest

Interest is money paid for the use of money borrowed or invested. Interest is calculated by using a formula. The simple interest formula has three important parts:
- Principal (p): amount of money borrowed or invested
- Rate of interest (r): written as a percent
- Time (t): figured in years

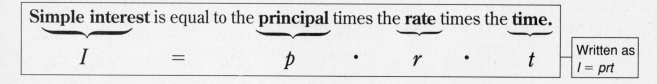

Simple interest is equal to the **principal** times the **rate** times the **time.**

$$I = p \cdot r \cdot t$$

Written as $I = prt$

Example

Dustin borrowed $545 to buy a new television. He was charged a 12% rate of interest. How much interest did he pay over 3 years?

Formula: $I = prt$

Replace known values: $I = p \cdot r \cdot t$

$545 \quad$ 12% or .12 $\quad$ 3

65.40 (3)

196.20

Solution: $196.20. The interest for 3 years was $196.20.

▶ Use the formula and the information given to solve the problems. Write the percent as a decimal or a fraction (for example, 8% = .08 = $\frac{8}{100}$).

1.

Alicia borrowed $320 for 2 years to purchase a desk. She was charged a 9% rate of interest. How much interest did she pay over 2 years?

a) _____
formula

b) _____
replace known values

c) The interest for 2 years was $ _____ .

2.

Jay deposited $800 in a new savings account at his local bank. At 7% interest, how much will he earn in 1 year?

a) _____
formula

b) _____
replace known values

c) Jay will earn $ _____ in interest.

Time, Rate, and Distance

When working with formulas, it is necessary to choose the proper formula to find the correct answer.

distance rate time
$$D = r \ t$$

rate distance
$$R = \frac{d}{t} \text{—time}$$

time distance
$$T = \frac{d}{r} \text{—rate}$$

Example

How fast must Joe drive if he has to travel 348 miles in 6 hours?

Step 1

Choose the proper formula.

The unknown is the rate of speed.

$$R = \frac{d}{t}$$

Step 2

Replace the variables with the values that are given.

$$R = \frac{d \text{—} 348}{t \text{—} 6}$$

Step 3

Solve to find the rate of speed.

$$R = \frac{348}{6}$$
$$R = 58$$

Joe must drive 58 mph.

▶ Choose the proper formula and solve. Label your answer in mph (speed), miles (distance), or hours (time).

1. At 63 mph, how many hours will it take to drive 189 miles?

a) _____ formula

b) _____ solution

2. How far will Manuel travel if he drives 47 mph for 8 hours?

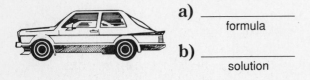

a) _____ formula

b) _____ solution

3. What speed must Denise drive to travel 416 miles in 8 hours?

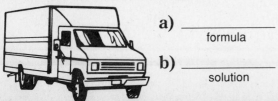

a) _____ formula

b) _____ solution

4. How long will it take to drive 192 miles if you average 48 mph?

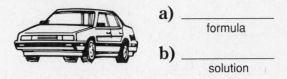

a) _____ formula

b) _____ solution

5. How fast must Michelle drive to travel 427 miles in 7 hours?

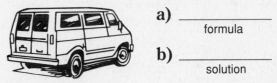

a) _____ formula

b) _____ solution

6. Rick has driven 5 hours at an average speed of 58 mph. How far has he traveled?

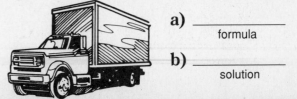

a) _____ formula

b) _____ solution

Geometric Formulas

When working with numbers, a formula is a great way to organize information.

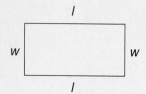

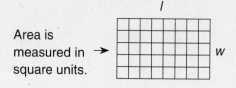

Area is measured in square units. →

Volume is measured in cubic units. →

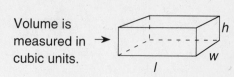

$P = l + l + w + w$
$\quad = 2l + 2w$

P = perimeter (the distance around a flat surface)
l = length
w = width

$A = lw$

A = area (the size of the surface)
l = length
w = width

$V = lwh$

V = volume (how much a solid figure can hold)
l = length
w = width
h = height

▶ Use the formulas above to solve the problems. Replace the variables with the numbers given in each problem.

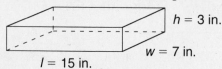

h = 3 in.
w = 7 in.
l = 15 in.

1. Find the volume of the solid.

a) _____ b) _____
    formula   fill in values

c) _____ cubic inches
  solution

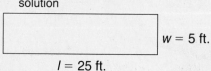

w = 5 ft.
l = 25 ft.

2. Find the area of the rectangle.

a) _____ b) _____
    formula   fill in values

c) _____ square feet
  solution

l = 35 ft.
w = 12 ft.

3. Find the perimeter of the rectangle.

a) _____ b) _____
    formula   fill in values

c) _____ feet
  solution

4. The Algrove family wants to carpet their living room. How many square feet (area) of carpet will be needed if the room is 28 feet long and 15 feet wide?

a) _____ b) _____
    formula   fill in values

c) _____ square feet
  solution

5. How many feet of fence will it take to go around (perimeter) a rectangular garden 20 feet long and 10 feet wide?

a) _____ b) _____
    formula   fill in values

c) _____ feet
  solution

6. How many cubic feet (volume) of storage space does a moving truck have? The dimensions are 17 feet long, 8 feet wide, and 9 feet high.

a) _____ b) _____
    formula   fill in values

c) _____ cubic feet
  solution

Learning about Ordered Pairs

When Mary attended a football game, she parked her car in the parking lot. The parking lot was labeled so people could remember where they parked. She wrote down C, 5 so she could find her car after the game.

For Mary to locate her car she would
• go to row C,
• then go to row 5.

The letter C tells Mary to go in one direction (right). The number 5 tells her to go in another direction (up).

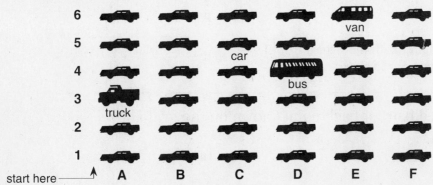

▶ Find each vehicle in the parking lot above.

1. Van

2. Truck

3. Bus

_____ , _____
letter   number

_____ , _____
letter   number

_____ , _____
letter   number

Suppose the letters across the bottom of the parking lot were replaced by numbers. The location of Mary's car is now 3, 5. (3 to the right and 5 up)

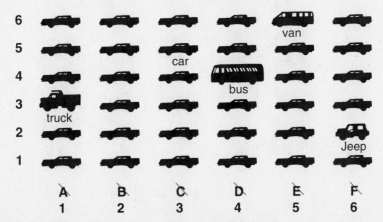

▶ Find each vehicle in the parking lot above using numbered pairs. Remember that the first number of each pair represents the bottom row of numbers.

4. Van _____ , _____
number   number

6. Truck _____ , _____
number   number

5. Bus _____ , _____
number   number

7. Jeep _____ , _____
number   number

More Ordered Pairs

Think of the parking lot on page 65 as a grid (shown below). An **ordered pair** of numbers (3, 6) can be graphed in the same way.

The first number always tells how many units on the horizontal axis.	The second number always tells how many units on the vertical axis.

Point A is (3, 6).

Start at the **origin** (0, 0) where the vertical axis and horizontal axis meet.

vertical axis

horizontal axis

▶ Name the ordered pair for each point shown on the grid above.

1. Point B (__7__ , _____)

2. Point C (_____ , __0__)

3. Point D (_____ , _____)

4. Point E (_____ , _____)

5. Point F (_____ , _____)

6. Point G (_____ , _____)

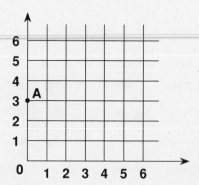

▶ Graph the ordered pairs on the grid above. The first one has been done for you.

7. A (0, 3)

8. B (5, 1)

9. C (2, 2)

10. D (4, 0)

11. E (1, 5)

12. F (0, 0)

Graphing Ordered Pairs

You can use positive and negative numbers to locate points on a grid.

- The first number of an ordered pair always tells how many units to the right (positive) or to the left (negative) of the origin.
- The second number always tells how many units up (positive) or down (negative) from the origin.
- The order of the numbers is important.

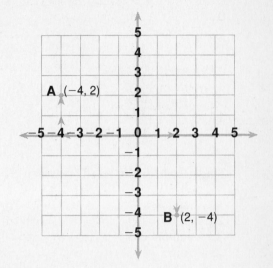

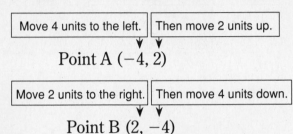

| Move 4 units to the left. | Then move 2 units up. |

Point A (−4, 2)

| Move 2 units to the right. | Then move 4 units down. |

Point B (2, −4)

▶ Name the ordered pair for each point shown on the grid. Remember to start counting at the origin.

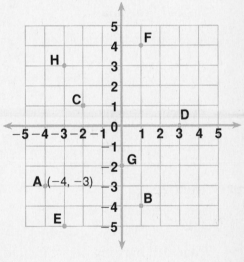

1. Point A (_−4_, _−3_)   **5.** Point E (____, ____)

2. Point B (____, ____)   **6.** Point F (____, ____)

3. Point C (____, ____)   **7.** Point G (____, ____)

4. Point D (____, _0_)   **8.** Point H (____, ____)

▶ Plot and label each point on the grid. The first one has been done for you.

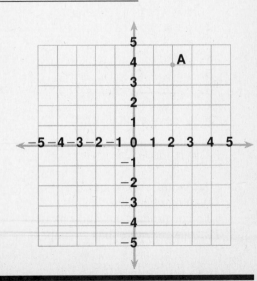

9. A (2, 4)   **13.** E (0, 5)

10. B (−2, 2)   **14.** F (4, 0)

11. C (5, −3)   **15.** G (2, −4)

12. D (−4, −2)   **16.** H (−3, 3)

ANSWER KEY

Page 1: Words to Expressions

1. $6 + 9$ Answers for 7–14 may vary.
2. $64 \div 8$
3. 6×4 7. Ten minus seven
4. $15 - 6$ 8. Nine times two
5. $15 + 20$ 9. Three more than four
6. $7 - 3$ 10. Fifteen divided by three
   11. The product of twenty and five
   12. Eighteen plus nine
   13. Fifty-six divided by eight
   14. The difference between thirteen and five

Page 2: Identify the Unknown

1. A number
2. Tax
3. A number
4. Refunds
5. A number
6. Judy's commission
7. Sale price
8. Options
9. Some number
10. A number

Page 3: Variables

Any variable may be used.

1. A number; $n - 3$
2. An amount; $w + 5$
3. Some number; $14 + n$
4. A number; $20 - n$
5. Mary's traveling time; $t + 1$
6. Some students; $10 + s$
7. Cost of a pencil; $c + \$.30$
8. A number; $n \div 9$
9. A weight; $w - 2$
10. A number; $5 \times n$

Page 4: Learning about Equations

1. $n + 4 = 5$
2. $6 = n + 3$
3. $n + 2 = 7$
4. $9 = n + 7$
5. $6 + n = 10$
6. $n - 6 = 3$
7. $9 \times n = 18$
8. $n \div 3 = 7$ or $\frac{n}{3} = 7$

Answers for 9–12 may vary.

9. A number plus 4 is 5.
10. A number minus 3 is 10.
11. The product of 4 and a number is 12.
12. 9 is one more than a number.

Page 5: Relating Addition and Subtraction

Numbers	Addition Equation	Subtraction Equation
1. 17, 4, 21	$\underline{17} + 4 = 21$	$21 - 4 = \underline{17}$
2. 11, 23, 34	$11 + 23 = \underline{34}$	$34 - 23 = \underline{11}$
3. 49, 22, 27	$27 + \underline{22} = \underline{49}$	$49 - \underline{27} = 22$
4. 12, 5, 7	$\underline{5} + \underline{7} = 12$	$\underline{12} - \underline{7} = 5$
5. 5, 9, 14	$\underline{5} + 9 = \underline{14}$	$14 - 9 = \underline{5}$
6. 76, 165, 89	$76 + \underline{89} = \underline{165}$	$165 - \underline{76} = 89$
7. 425, 138, 287	$\underline{287} + 138 = \underline{425}$	$425 - 138 = \underline{287}$

8. $4 + 6 = 10$ or $6 + 4 = 10$
   $10 - 6 = 4$ or $10 - 4 = 6$
9. $7 + 15 = 22$ or $15 + 7 = 22$
   $22 - 7 = 15$ or $22 - 15 = 7$
10. $10 + 20 = 30$ or $20 + 10 = 30$
    $30 - 10 = 20$ or $30 - 20 = 10$
11. $64 + 37 = 101$ or $37 + 64 = 101$
    $101 - 64 = 37$ or $101 - 37 = 64$

Page 6: Equations and Balance Scales

1. $x + 6 = 9$
2. $6 = n + 3$
3. $y + 4 = 5$
4. $7 = x + 2$

Page 7: Solving Equations

1. a) $n + 4 = 9$
   b) 4
   c) 4
   d) $n = 5$

2. a) $8 = y + 3$
   b) 3
   c) 3
   d) $y = 5$

3. a) $a + 2 = 10$
   b) 2
   c) 2
   d) $a = 8$

4. a) $6 = x + 5$
   b) 5
   c) 5
   d) $x = 1$

5. $y = 3$
6. $9 = x$
7. $a = 4$
8. $4 = t$

Page 8: Inverse Operations

1. 8
2. 18
3. 16
4. 51
5. 88
6. 19
7. 52
8. 17
9. 49
10. 152

Page 9: Solving Equations by Adding or Subtracting

1. $y - 8 = 21$
$+ 8 + 8$
$\overline{y = 29}$

2. $a + 19 = 42$
$- 19 - 19$
$\overline{a = 23}$

3. $28 = b - 13$
$+ 13 + 13$
$\overline{41 = b}$

4. $c - 17 = 35$
$+ 17 + 17$
$\overline{c = 52}$

5. $61 = x + 37$
$- 37 - 37$
$\overline{24 = x}$

6. $46 = x + 29$
$- 29 - 29$
$\overline{17 = x}$

7. $a + 17 = 31$
$- 17 - 17$
$\overline{a = 14}$

8. $132 = a - 58$
$+ 58 + 58$
$\overline{190 = a}$

Page 10: Equations to Add or Subtract

1. $x - 7 = 15$
$+ 7 + 7$
$\overline{x = 22}$

Check:
$x - 7 = 15$
$22 - 7 = 15$
$15 = 15$

2. $30 + t = 93$
$- 30 - 30$
$\overline{t = 63}$

Check:
$30 + t = 93$
$30 + 63 = 93$
$93 = 93$

3. $a + 128 = 314$
$- 128 - 128$
$\overline{a = 186}$

Check:
$a + 128 = 314$
$186 + 128 = 314$
$314 = 314$

4. $50 = h - 18$
$+ 18 + 18$
$\overline{68 = h}$

Check:
$50 = h - 18$
$50 = 68 - 18$
$50 = 50$

5. $84 = r + 28$
$- 28 - 28$
$\overline{56 = r}$

Check:
$84 = r + 28$
$84 = 56 + 28$
$84 = 84$

6. $x - 172 = 86$
$+ 172 + 172$
$\overline{x = 258}$

Check:
$x - 172 = 86$
$258 - 172 = 86$
$86 = 86$

7. $500 = b - 50$
$+ 50 + 50$
$\overline{550 = b}$

Check:
$500 = b - 50$
$500 = 550 - 50$
$500 = 500$

8. $n + 316 = 648$
$- 316 - 316$
$\overline{n = 332}$

Check:
$n + 316 = 648$
$332 + 316 = 648$
$648 = 648$

Page 11: Sentences to Equations

1. a) $x - 15 = 9$
   b) $x = 24$

2. a) $n + 59 = 101$
   b) $n = 42$

3. a) $x + 65 = 421$
   b) $x = 356$

4. a) $y - 17 = 71$
   b) $y = 88$

5. a) $c + 135 = 211$
   b) $c = 76$

Any variable may be used in 6–10.

6. a) n
   b) $n - 53 = 27$
   c) $n = 80$

7. a) x
   b) $x + 138 = 221$
   c) $x = 83$

8. a) n
   b) $n + 84 = 128$
   c) $n = 44$

9. a) n
   b) $n - 39 = 15$
   c) $n = 54$

10. a) y
    b) $y - 118 = 56$
    c) $y = 174$

Page 12: Relating Multiplication and Division

Numbers	Multiplication Equation	Division Equation
1. 9, 8, 72	$\underline{9} \times 8 = 72$	$72 \div \underline{9} = 8$
2. 39, 13, 3	$13 \times \underline{3} = 39$	$\underline{39} \div 13 = \underline{3}$
3. 15, 105, 7	$15 \times 7 = \underline{105}$	$105 \div \underline{15} = 7$
4. 4, 20, 80	$4 \times \underline{20} = 80$	$80 \div \underline{20} = 4$
5. 174, 6, 29	$29 \times \underline{6} = 174$	$\underline{174} \div 29 = \underline{6}$
6. 8, 88, 11	$8 \times \underline{11} = \underline{88}$	$88 \div \underline{11} = 8$
7. 48, 6, 8	$\underline{6} \times 8 = \underline{48}$	$\underline{48} \div 8 = \underline{6}$

8. $28 \div 7 = 4$ or $28 \div 4 = 7$
9. $8 \times 5 = 40$
10. $3 \times 7 = 21$ or $7 \times 3 = 21$
$21 \div 3 = 7$ or $21 \div 7 = 3$
11. $5 \times 9 = 45$ or $9 \times 5 = 45$
$45 \div 5 = 9$ or $45 \div 9 = 5$
12. $12 \times 9 = 108$ or $9 \times 12 = 108$
$108 \div 12 = 9$ or $108 \div 9 = 12$
13. $10 \times 8 = 80$ or $8 \times 10 = 80$
$80 \div 10 = 8$ or $80 \div 8 = 10$

Page 13: Solving Equations by Dividing

1. 4
2. 8
3. 12
4. 25

5. $\dfrac{\cancel{3}c}{\cancel{3}} = \dfrac{111}{3}$
$c = 37$

6. $\dfrac{90}{15} = \dfrac{\cancel{15}y}{\cancel{15}}$
$6 = y$

Page 13: Solving Equations by Dividing (continued)

7. $\dfrac{\cancel{4}x}{\cancel{4}} = \dfrac{120}{4}$
$x = 30$

9. $\dfrac{\cancel{20}n}{\cancel{20}} = \dfrac{800}{20}$
$n = 40$

8. $\dfrac{156}{13} = \dfrac{\cancel{13}h}{\cancel{13}}$
$12 = h$

10. $\dfrac{\cancel{9}x}{\cancel{9}} = \dfrac{171}{9}$
$x = 19$

Page 14: Solving Equations by Multiplying

1. 3
2. 3
3. 11
4. 18

5. $\cancel{9} \cdot \dfrac{n}{\cancel{9}} = 6 \cdot 9$
$n = 54$

6. $7 \cdot 5 = \dfrac{a}{\cancel{7}} \cdot \cancel{7}$
$35 = a$

7. $\cancel{12} \cdot \dfrac{x}{\cancel{12}} = 3 \cdot 12$
$x = 36$

8. $8 \cdot 13 = \dfrac{c}{\cancel{8}} \cdot \cancel{8}$
$104 = c$

9. $\cancel{22} \cdot \dfrac{r}{\cancel{22}} = 5 \cdot 22$
$r = 110$

10. $\cancel{15} \cdot \dfrac{h}{\cancel{15}} = 22 \cdot 15$
$h = 330$

Page 15: Equations to Multiply or Divide

1. $\dfrac{\cancel{6}r}{\cancel{6}} = \dfrac{138}{6}$
$r = 23$

Check:
$6r = 138$
$6 \cdot 23 = 138$
$138 = 138$

2. $7 \cdot 8 = \dfrac{m}{\cancel{7}} \cdot \cancel{7}$
$56 = m$

Check:
$8 = \dfrac{m}{7}$
$8 = \dfrac{56}{7}$
$8 = 8$

3. $\dfrac{350}{25} = \dfrac{\cancel{25}h}{\cancel{25}}$
$14 = h$

Check:
$350 = 25h$
$350 = 25 \cdot 14$
$350 = 350$

4. $\cancel{7} \cdot \dfrac{n}{\cancel{7}} = 16 \cdot 7$
$n = 112$

Check:
$\dfrac{n}{7} = 16$
$\dfrac{112}{7} = 16$
$16 = 16$

5. $\dfrac{\cancel{21}c}{\cancel{21}} = \dfrac{168}{21}$
$c = 8$

Check:
$21c = 168$
$21 \cdot 8 = 168$
$168 = 168$

6. $3 \cdot 124 = \dfrac{w}{\cancel{3}} \cdot \cancel{3}$
$372 = w$

Check:
$124 = \dfrac{w}{3}$
$124 = \dfrac{372}{3}$
$124 = 124$

7. $\cancel{9} \cdot \dfrac{u}{\cancel{9}} = 9 \cdot 9$
$u = 81$

Check:
$\dfrac{u}{9} = 9$
$\dfrac{81}{9} = 9$
$9 = 9$

Page 15: Equations to Multiply or Divide (continued)

8. $\dfrac{374}{11} = \dfrac{\cancel{11}s}{\cancel{11}}$
$34 = s$

Check:
$374 = 11s$
$374 = 11 \cdot 34$
$374 = 374$

Page 16: Word Statements to Equations

1. a) $8m = 96$
b) 12

2. a) $78 = 6r$
b) $r = 13$

3. a) $\dfrac{x}{13} = 4$
b) $x = 52$

4. a) $7 = \dfrac{t}{25}$
b) $t = 175$

5. a) $18n = 126$
b) $n = 7$

Any variable may be used in 6–9.

6. a) n
b) $8n = 152$
c) $n = 19$

7. a) n
b) $\dfrac{n}{15} = 75$
c) $n = 1{,}125$

8. a) n
b) $135 = \dfrac{n}{9}$
c) $1{,}215 = n$

9. a) n
b) $23n = 253$
c) $n = 11$

Page 17: Proportion

1. a) $\dfrac{\$55 \text{ saved}}{5 \text{ weeks}} = \dfrac{n \text{ saved}}{7 \text{ weeks}}$
b) $385 = 5n$
c) $\$77 = n$

2. a) $\dfrac{64 \text{ miles}}{2 \text{ gallons}} = \dfrac{n \text{ miles}}{9 \text{ gallons}}$
b) $576 = 2n$
c) $288 \text{ miles} = n$

Page 18: Proportions in Problem Solving

A reverse setup of the proportions would also be correct.

1. a) $\dfrac{6 \text{ pounds}}{6{,}500 \text{ square feet}} = \dfrac{9 \text{ pounds}}{n \text{ square feet}}$
b) $6n = 58{,}500$
c) $n = 9{,}750 \text{ square feet}$

2. a) $\dfrac{4 \text{ eggs}}{48 \text{ doughnuts}} = \dfrac{n \text{ eggs}}{120 \text{ doughnuts}}$
b) $480 = 48n$
c) $10 \text{ eggs} = n$

3. a) $\dfrac{13 \text{ ounces}}{\$3.12 \text{ cost}} = \dfrac{20 \text{ ounces}}{n \text{ cost}}$
b) $13n = \$62.40$
c) $n = \$4.80$

4. a) $\dfrac{7 \text{ gallons}}{196 \text{ miles}} = \dfrac{n \text{ gallons}}{532 \text{ miles}}$
b) $3{,}724 = 196n$
c) $19 \text{ gallons} = n$

Page 19: Mixed Practice

1. $m = 75$
2. $168 = b$
3. $s = 158$
4. $w = 16$
5. $w = 66$
6. $n = 64$

Page 19: Mixed Practice (continued)

7. a) $\frac{2 \text{ pounds}}{24 \text{ minutes}} = \frac{5 \text{ pounds}}{n \text{ minutes}}$

b) $2n = 120$

c) $n = 60$ minutes

8. a) $\frac{1 \text{ tablespoon}}{8 \text{ ounces}} = \frac{n \text{ tablespoons}}{64 \text{ ounces}}$

b) $64 = 8n$

c) $8 = n$

9. a) $\frac{26 \text{ miles}}{1 \text{ gallon}} = \frac{n \text{ miles}}{12 \text{ gallons}}$

b) $312 = 1n$

c) $312 = n$

Page 20: Define a Variable

Any variable may be used.

1. a) Amount of weight Andy lost

b) Let w = the amount of weight Andy lost.

c) Any two of the following:

$185 + w = 207$

$w + 185 = 207$

$w = 207 - 185$

d) $w = 22$ pounds

2. a) Amount of money in Janet's checking account

b) Let m = the amount of money in Janet's checking account.

c) Any two of the following:

$\$182.07 - \$43.56 = m$

$\$43.56 + m = \$182.07$

$m + \$43.56 = \$182.07$

d) $m = \$138.51$

Page 21: Problem-Solving Skills

Any variable may be used. Equation setups may vary.

1. a) let n = the number

b) $9n = 108$

c) $n = 12$

2. a) let n = the number

b) $n - \$33 = \$18$

c) $n = \$51$

3. a) let n = the number

b) $\frac{n}{6} = 15$

c) $n = 90$

4. a) let n = the original price

b) $n - \$15 = \$18$

c) $n = \$33$

5. a) let n = how much Roberto earned per hour

b) $32n = \$352$

c) $n = \$11$

6. a) let n = how many cassette tapes Gregg bought

b) $\$8n = \$48$

c) $n = 6$

Page 22: Two-Step Equations Using a Balance Scale

1. a) $3n + 2 = 8$ **c)** $3n = 6$ **e)** 2

b) 2   **d)** 3

Page 23: Picture the Equations

Page 24: Solving Two-Step Equations

1. a) Subtract 6 from each side.

b) Divide each side by 4.

2. a) Add 5 to each side.

b) Divide each side by 2.

3. a) Add 7 to each side.

b) Divide each side by 8.

4. a) Subtract 4 from each side.

b) Divide each side by 5.

5. $4x + 3 = 15$

$\underline{\quad -3 \quad -3}$

$4x \quad\quad = 12$

$\frac{4x}{4} \quad = \frac{12}{4}$

$x = 3$

6. $6n - 10 = 32$

$\underline{\quad\quad + 10 + 10}$

$6n \quad\quad = 42$

$\frac{6n}{6} \quad = \frac{42}{6}$

$n = 7$

7. $9x - 8 = 37$

$\underline{\quad\quad + 8 \ + 8}$

$9x \quad\quad = 45$

$\frac{9x}{9} \quad = \frac{45}{9}$

$x = 5$

8. $12y + 10 = 70$

$\underline{\quad\quad - 10 - 10}$

$12y \quad\quad = 60$

$\frac{12y}{12} \quad = \frac{60}{12}$

$y = 5$

Page 25: More Two-Step Equations

1. a) Add 1 to each side.
b) Multiply each side by 4.

2. a) Subtract 9 from each side.
b) Multiply each side by 2.

3. a) Add 7 to each side.
b) Multiply each side by 3.

4. a) Subtract 3 from each side.
b) Multiply each side by 7.

5. $n = 36$
6. $x = 88$

7. $y = 90$
8. $a = 48$

Page 26: Checking Two-Step Equations

1. $n = 9$ Check:
$$3n + 15 = 42$$
$$3 \cdot 9 + 15 = 42$$
$$27 + 15 = 42$$
$$42 = 42$$

2. $t = 7$ Check:
$$5t - 6 = 29$$
$$5 \cdot 7 - 6 = 29$$
$$35 - 6 = 29$$
$$29 = 29$$

3. $h = 132$ Check:
$$\frac{h}{12} - 4 = 7$$
$$\frac{132}{12} - 4 = 7$$
$$11 - 4 = 7$$
$$7 = 7$$

4. $n = 11$ Check:
$$2n - 9 = 13$$
$$2 \cdot 11 - 9 = 13$$
$$22 - 9 = 13$$
$$13 = 13$$

5. $x = 24$ Check:
$$\frac{x}{2} - 6 = 6$$
$$\frac{24}{2} - 6 = 6$$
$$12 - 6 = 6$$
$$6 = 6$$

6. $a = 0$ Check:
$$7a + 3 = 3$$
$$7 \cdot 0 + 3 = 3$$
$$0 + 3 = 3$$
$$3 = 3$$

7. $y = 9$ Check:
$$\frac{y}{3} + 9 = 12$$
$$\frac{9}{3} + 9 = 12$$
$$3 + 9 = 12$$
$$12 = 12$$

Page 26: Checking Two-Step Equations (continued)

Check:
8. $m = 6$
$$4m + 19 = 43$$
$$4 \cdot 6 + 19 = 43$$
$$24 + 19 = 43$$
$$43 = 43$$

Page 27: Translating Word Statements

Any variable may be used.

1. a) Let n = a number.
b) $4n + 3 = 23$

2. a) Let n = a number.
b) $\frac{n}{9} + 5 = 7$

3. a) Let n = a number.
b) $2n + 15 = 29$

4. a) Let n = a number.
b) $5 = \frac{n}{4} - 10$

5. D
6. A
7. C
8. B

Page 28: More Problem Solving

Any variable may be used.

1. a) Let n = the price of each skirt.
b) $2n + 22 = 58$
c) $n = \$18$

2. a) Let n = the price of each tire.
b) $5n + 15 = 240$
c) $n = \$45$

3. a) Let n = Mike's wages for each week.
b) $4n + 150 = 1{,}250$
c) $n = \$275$

4. a) Let n = the price of each ticket.
b) $3n + 4 = 82$
c) $n = \$26$

Page 29: Review Your Skills

1. $t = 36$
2. $s = 80$
3. $m = 13$
4. $n = 8$
5. $a = 64$
6. $x = 66$
7. $n = 6$
8. $y = 18$

Any variable may be used in 9–12.

9. a) $n + 38 = 102$
b) $n = 64$

10. a) $414 \div 46 = w$
b) $w = \$9$

11. a) $2m + 12 = 48$
b) $m = 18$

12. a) $\frac{n}{5} - 9 = 2$
b) $n = 55$

Page 30: Negative and Positive Numbers

1. +7
2. −3
3. +5
4. +$8
5. −20
6. −4
7. +5
8. +$75
9. −5
10. −$15

Page 31: Use the Number Line

1. +3
2. −6
3. −15
4. +7
5. −1
6. −5
7. −6, −5, <u>−4</u>, <u>−3</u>, −2, <u>−1</u>, 0, <u>+1</u>, <u>+2</u>, +3
8. +6, +5, <u>+4</u>, <u>+3</u>, +2, <u>+1</u>, 0, −1, <u>−2</u>, <u>−3</u>, <u>−4</u>
9. −6, −4, <u>−2</u>, 0, <u>+2</u>, <u>+4</u>, +6, <u>+8</u>, <u>+10</u>, +12
10. −14, −11, <u>−8</u>, <u>−5</u>, −2, <u>+1</u>, <u>+4</u>, <u>+7</u>, +10

Page 32: Comparing and Ordering Integers

1. a) >   c) >   e) <
   b) <   d) >   f) <

2. a) 0   c) 8   e) −37
   b) −5   d) 2   f) 15

3. a) −4   c) −1   e) −8
   b) −9   d) −13   f) 21

4. a) −4, −1, 0, 3, 5
   b) −10, −4, 3, 5, 8

Page 33: Adding Integers with the Same Sign

1. −4 + (−5) = −9   5. 16   8. −10
2. 3 + 4 = 7   6. −25   9. −109
3. −3 + (−6) = −9   7. 21   10. 132
4. −10

Page 34: Adding Integers with Different Signs

1. 2

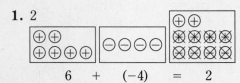

    6 + (−4) = 2

2. −5

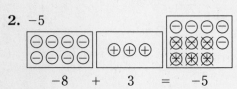

    −8 + 3 = −5

3. 5   5. 3   7. −6   9. −58
4. −6   6. −3   8. 9   10. 58

Page 35: Absolute Value

1. a) 5   d) 3   2. a   5. c
   b) 8   e) 25   3. a   6. 10
   c) 9   f) 4   4. b   7. 13

Page 35: Absolute Value (continued)

8. 16   10. 4   12. 17
9. 24   11. 4   13. 3

Page 36: Rules for Adding Integers

1. a) − (negative)   5. a) + (positive)
   b) −5   b) 9

2. a) − (negative)   6. a) + (positive)
   b) −43   b) 25

3. a) − (negative)   7. a) − (negative)
   b) −8   b) −68

4. a) + (positive)   8. a) + (positive)
   b) 11   b) 980

Page 37: Subtracting Integers with the Same Sign

1. −2   2. 6   3. −3

4. −4   7. 12   9. −139
5. 5   8. −184   10. 821
6. −23

Page 38: Relating Subtraction to Addition

1.

a) −2   b) −2
c) 3

2.

a) −4   b) −4
c) −2

3.

a) −1   b) −1
c) −4, +4

Page 39: Using Opposites

1. +4   5. +30   9. a) 8
2. −4   6. −30   b) −7
3. −7   7. +5   c) 15
4. +7   8. −5   d) −5

Page 39: Using Opposites (continued)

10. $-5 + 3$
11. $-8 + (-9)$
12. $11 + 7$
13. $-8 + (-22)$
14. $35 + 13$
15. $47 + (-15)$

Page 40: Rules for Subtracting Integers

1. $9 + (-4) = 5$
2. $-7 + (+2) = -5$
3. $8 + (+10) = 18$
4. $3 + (-20) = -17$
5. $-11 + (-2) = -13$
6. $-19 + (+5) = -14$
7. $56 + (+13) = 69$
8. $27 + (-52) = -25$
9. $14 + (-6) = 8$
10. $195 + (+459) = 654$

Page 41: Adding and Subtracting Integers

1. 7
2. 24
3. -6
4. -45
5. 11
6. 11
7. 63
8. -17
9. 12
10. -16
11. 114
12. 0
13. 167
14. -13
15. -961
16. -501

Page 42: Applications Using Integers

1. 8 degrees
2. $29°$
3. 5 yards were gained
4. $-16 + (-24) = -40, 40$
5. $69 - 75 = -\$6, -\$6$

Page 43: Multiplying Integers with Different Signs

1. -40
2. -48
3. -45
4. -70
5. -375
6. -132
7. $-1,271$
8. $-5,040$

Page 44: Multiplying Integers with the Same Sign

1. 75
2. 84
3. 234
4. 1,764
5. 126
6. 100
7. 125
8. 44
9. 60
10. 63
11. 21
12. 768
13. 76
14. 72
15. 375
16. 110
17. 96
18. 350
19. 1,000
20. 5,700

Page 45: Multiplying Integers

1. Negative
2. Positive
3. Negative
4. Positive
5. a) $-$
   b) -77
6. a) $+$
   b) 45
7. a) $+$
   b) 60
8. a) $-$
   b) -48
9. a) $-$
   b) -24
10. a) $+$
    b) 531
11. a) $-$
    b) -700
12. a) $+$
    b) 820
13. a) $+$
    b) 360
14. a) $-$
    b) $-7,749$

Page 46: Dividing Integers with Different Signs

1. a) $-5, -$
   b) $-6, -$
   c) $-8, -$
   d) $-2, -$
2. -4
3. -36
4. -9
5. -9
6. -7
7. -3
8. -9
9 -11

Page 47: Dividing Integers with the Same Sign

1. a) $3, +$
   b) $4, +$
   c) $9, +$
   d) $8, +$
2. 9
3. 5
4. 4
5. 14
6. 5
7. 65
8. 7
9. 13

Page 48: Dividing Integers

1. Positive
2. Positive
3. Negative
4. Negative
5. a) $-$
   b) -3
6. a) $-$
   b) -6
7. a) $+$
   b) 7
8. a) $+$
   b) 7
9. a) $-$
   b) -4
10. a) $+$
    b) 34
11. a) $-$
    b) -15
12. a) $+$
    b) 18
13. a) $+$
    b) 15
14. a) $-$
    b) -8

Page 49: Review of Integers

1. -525
2. -49
3. -22
4. -5
5. -42
6. 176
7. 31
8. -19
9. $-60 < 60$
10. $7 > -17$
11. $8 > -18$
12. $40 > 39$
13. $-44 < 45$
14. $-25 < 15$
15. $-34 < -6$
16. $-48 < 77$

Page 50: Applications Using Integers

1. $-5 \times 4 = -20, 20$
2. $-64 \div 4 = -16, 16$
3. $315 \div 5 = 63, 63$
4. $-425 \times 5 = -2,125, \$2,125$
5. $45 \times 8 = 360, 360$

Page 51: Multistep Problems Using Integers

1. a) $128 \div 16 = 8$ minutes
   b) $45 - (2 \times 8) = 29$ minutes
2. a) $4 \times \$225 = \$900$
   b) $\$1,215 - \$900 = \$315$
3. a) $\$875 - \$490 = \$385$
   b) $\$385 + \$326 = \$711$
4. a) $4 \times 6 = 24°$
   b) $17 - 24 = -7°$
5. a) $\$4,580 + (-\$9,450) = -\$4,870$
   b) $\$2,460 + \$4,870 = \$7,330$

Page 52: Learning Order of Operations

1. $(-8)(-5)(2)$

$\quad\quad (40)(2)$

$\quad\quad\quad 80$

3. $(-6)(-4)(-2)$

$\quad\quad (24)(-2)$

$\quad\quad\quad -48$

2. $28 - (-7) + 8$

$\quad\quad 35 + 8$

$\quad\quad\quad 43$

4. -3
5. -378
6. -3
7. 90
8. -11
9. 31
10. -240

Page 53: Ordering Expressions

1. $(5)(-4) + 9$

$\quad -20 + 9 = -11$

4. $12 - (3)(-2) + 9$

$\quad 12 - \quad (-6) \quad + 9 = 27$

2. $-4 + (6)(5)$

$\quad -4 + \quad 30 = 26$

5. 40
6. 39
7. 51
8. 25
9. 16
10. -2

3. $17 + 10 \div 2$

$\quad 17 + \quad 5 = 22$

Page 54: Simplify the Expression

1. $3(-2) - (3 + 1)$

$\quad 3(-2) - \quad 4$

$\quad -6 - 4 = -10$

3. $5[9 + (-15) - 3]$

$\quad\quad 5 \quad (-9) = -45$

4. -6
5. -5
6. 30
7. 12
8. 5
9. -9
10. 4

2. $25 - 3(5 - 3)$

$\quad 25 - 3 \quad (2)$

$\quad 25 - 6 = 19$

Page 55: Using Order of Operation

1. a
2. b
3. b
4. a
5. c
6. a
7. b
8. b

9. $(3 + 9) \div (3 - 1) = 6$
10. $3 \times (6 + 4) \div 2 = 15$
11. $(7 + 2) \times 3 + 4 = 31$
12. $30 \div (6 + 4) \times 5 = 15$
13. $12 \boxplus 7 \boxminus 3 = 16$
14. $(6 \boxplus 4) \boxtimes 3 = 30$
15. $(-15) \boxdiv 5 \boxplus (-4) = -7$
16. $30 \boxminus 4 \boxtimes (8 \boxminus 2) = 6$

Page 56: Exponents

	Expression	Base	Exponent	Meaning	Value
1.	3^2	3	2	$(3)(3)$	9
2.	$(-2)^5$	-2	5	$(-2)(-2)(-2)(-2)(-2)$	-32
3.	5^4	5	4	$(5)(5)(5)(5)$	625
4.	2^6	2	6	$(2)(2)(2)(2)(2)(2)$	64
5.	$(-4)^4$	-4	4	$(-4)(-4)(-4)(-4)$	256
6.	$(-3)^3$	-3	3	$(-3)(-3)(-3)$	-27
7.	10^3	10	3	$(10)(10)(10)$	1,000

8. $3^3 = 27$
9. $5^2 = 25$
10. $2^4 = 16$
11. $2^2 = 4$
12. $3^2 = 9$
13. $5^3 = 125$

Page 57: Evaluate Expressions

1. $15 + 3$

$\quad\quad 18$

2. $20 \div (-2)$

$\quad\quad -10$

3. $5(1) + (-2)$

$\quad\quad 5 + (-2)$

$\quad\quad\quad 3$

4. -5
5. -5
6. -6
7. 2
8. -9
9. 5
10. -3

Page 58: Evaluate with Exponents

1. $4(2) + (3)(3)$

$\quad 8 + 9$

$\quad\quad 17$

2. $5(-2)(-2)(-2)$

$\quad\quad -40$

3. $(3)(3) - (-2)(-2)(-2)$

$\quad\quad 9 \quad - \quad (-8)$

$\quad\quad\quad\quad 17$

4. 10
5. 15
6. 11
7. -36
8. -10
9. 9
10. 14

Page 59: Review Your Skills

1. 11
2. −3
3. 4
4. −39
5. −5
6. −36
7. 7
8. −91
9. $3 \boxtimes 5 \boxplus 9 = 24$
10. $(17 \boxplus 3) \boxdiv (−5) = −4$
11. $13 \boxminus 7 \boxplus (−1) = 5$
12. 16
13. 2
14. 81

Any variable may be used in 15–24.

15. $n + 15$
16. $9n$
17. $35 − n$
18. $\frac{n}{6}$
19. 7
20. 11
21. −12
22. 15
23. 77
24. −6

Page 60: Learning about Formulas

1. $I = prt$
2. $T = 20w$
3. $C = p + t$
4. $A = lw$

Answers for 5–8 may vary.

5. The total cost is equal to the number of units bought times the price of one unit.
6. The area of a triangle is equal to one-half times the length of the base times the height of the triangle.
7. The perimeter of a square is equal to four times the length of one side.
8. The percent score of a 20-point quiz is equal to one hundred minus five times the number of wrong answers.

Page 61: Using Formulas

1. $T = 35w$
   $T = (35)(10)$
   $T = 350$ minutes

2. $T = 35w$
   $T = (35)(16)$
   $T = 560$ minutes

3. $C = np + t$
   $C = 3(1.79) + .32$
   $C = \$5.69$

4. $C = np + t$
   $C = 2(2.89) + .35$
   $C = \$6.13$

Page 62: Simple Interest

1. a) $I = prt$ ⬜ 9%
   b) $I = (\$320)(.09)(2)$
   c) The interest for 2 years was \$57.60.

2. a) $I = prt$ ⬜ 7%
   b) $I = (800)(.07)(\times 1)$
   c) Jay will earn \$56 in interest.

Page 63: Time, Rate, and Distance

1. a) $T = \frac{d}{r}$
   b) $T = 3$ hours
2. a) $D = rt$
   b) $D = 376$ miles
3. a) $R = \frac{d}{t}$
   b) $R = 52$ mph

4. a) $T = \frac{d}{r}$
   b) $T = 4$ hours
5. a) $R = \frac{d}{t}$
   b) $R = 61$ mph
6. a) $D = rt$
   b) $D = 290$ miles

Page 64: Geometric Formulas

1. a) $V = lwh$
   b) $V = (15)(7)(3)$
   c) $V = 315$ cubic inches

2. a) $A = lw$
   b) $A = (25)(5)$
   c) $A = 125$ square feet

3. a) $P = 2l + 2w$
   b) $P = 2(35) + 2(12)$
   c) $P = 94$ feet

4. a) $A = lw$
   b) $A = (28)(15)$
   c) $A = 420$ square feet

5. a) $P = 2l + 2w$
   b) $P = 2(20) + 2(10)$
   c) $P = 60$ feet

6. a) $V = lwh$
   b) $V = (17)(8)(9)$
   c) $V = 1,224$ cubic feet

Page 65: Learning about Ordered Pairs

1. E, 6
2. A, 3
3. D, 4
4. 5, 6
5. 4, 4
6. 1, 3
7. 6, 2

Page 66: More Ordered Pairs

1. (7, 3)
2. (2, 0)
3. (0, 4)
4. (6, 7)
5. (4, 2)
6. (5, 5)

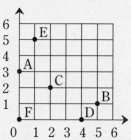

Page 67: Graphing Ordered Pairs

1. Point A (−4, −3)
2. Point B (1, −4)
3. Point C (−2, 1)
4. Point D (3, 0)
5. Point E (−3, −5)
6. Point F (1, 4)
7. Point G (0, −2)
8. Point H (−3, 3)

9–16: Refer to graph.

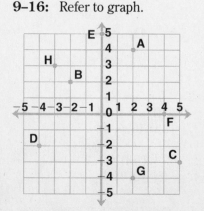